FORGOTTEN BEACONS

FORGOTTEN BEACONS

The Lost Lighthouses of the Chesapeake Bay

Patrick Hornberger & Linda Turbyville

EASTWIND PUBLISHING

ANNAPOLIS, MARYLAND

Published by Eastwind Publishing
Annapolis, Maryland U.S.A.

For information about permission to
reproduce selections from this book write to the publisher,
Eastwind Publishing, P.O.Box 1773, Annapolis, MD 21404. 410-721-7987

Hornberger, Patrick & Turbyville, Linda

Forgotten Beacons
The Lost Lighthouses of the Chesapeake Bay

Includes bibliographical reference and index

ISBN 1-885457-09-X

Second Edition

Printed in the United States

Cover photo of Blackistone Island lighthouse courtesy of the Mariners' Musuem

ACKNOWLEDGMENTS

Many people have given generously of their time and expertise to answer questions, to help in the location of photographic material and to guide us through archival materials.

We would especially like to thank members of the U.S. Coast Guard, including, R. M. Browning, Jr., Historian, U.S. Coast Guard Headquarters, Washington, D.C.; Lieutenant Edward A. Westfall, Lighthouse Program Manager, and John Walters, Chief, Aids to Navigation, U.S. Coast Guard Fifth District, Portsmouth, Virginia; Dottie Mitchell, U.S. Coast Guard Yard, Curtis Bay, Baltimore, Maryland; and Cindy Herrick, Coast Guard Academy, New London, Connecticut.

It is indeed fortunate that we have the presence and excellence of the Chesapeake Bay's several regional museums and we thank the curators and their staff for patience and grace in answering questions and locating materials. We would especially like to thank Pete Lesher, Curator, Chesapeake Maritime Museum, St. Michael's, Maryland; Richard J. Dodds, Curator of Maritime History, Calvert Marine Museum, Solomons, Maryland; Alice C. Hanes, Curator, Naval Shipyard Museum, Lightship Portsmouth, Portsmouth, Virginia; and Claudia McFall, Photographic Services, and the archival staff of the Mariners' Museum, Newport News, Virginia.

We regret we cannot present all we have learned and gained from this research and remind the reader that we are responsible for any oversights and omissions.

≈

We have especially missed the encouragement and broad knowledge of Herb Entwistle, longtime president of the Chesapeake Chapter of the United States Lighthouse Society, who died while this volume was in preparation. We would like to dedicate this volume to our lost colleague, to his family and many friends who will, we are certain, remember him whenever they approach a lighthouse on the Bay.

CONTENTS

IMPORTANT NOTES

Readers should understand that this book does not include information in any detail on the Chesapeake Bay's standing lighthouses or that station's previous structure or lightships. Information on those lighthouses may be found in Eastwind Publishing's companion title, *BAY BEACONS*, *Lighthouses of the Chesapeake Bay*, by Linda Turbyville. Together, these books will give the reader a complete history of lighthouses and lightships on the Chesapeake Bay.

Second, it is important for the reader to remember that lighthouses and lightships, as established by the early U.S. lighthouse establishments or the U.S. Coast Guard, were created as *stations*. This book is an outline of the stations once having a lighthouse structure or ship on location on the Chesapeake Bay. Headings giving three dates are stations originally established by a lightship—the first date being the date of the first lightship—the second date, that of the first lighthouse, and the third, the date of the decommissioning or dismantling of the lighthouse. Any number of structures or ships could be on a station over a period of time. Every effort was made by the authors to present a complete illustrative history and most, but not all, structures or ships placed on a station are shown in this book.

Third, the date of a lighthouse station's actual commissioning (lighting) may come months—even years—after the lighthouse station is authorized by Congress or the date that congressional appropriations are received. Similarly, automation may come years before a lighthouse is decommissioned and may even retain a keeper for a time. Finally, many lighthouses remained in place for years after they were decommissioned before being demolished or dismantled. These notable dates in a lighthouse's history may appear to cause some discrepancies in the dates assigned to particular lighthouse stations.

INTRODUCTION

Behind the sentimentality of local lighthouse lore lies the real magic of the Chesapeake Bay, enigmatic and ever-changing, inviting the adventurous and world-weary alike to more familiar acquaintance. The Bay offers many identifiable landmarks, including thirty-four well-loved lighthouses that have weathered time, the elements, some curious technological innovations, and the larger transformations of American society. It is difficult to believe that these remaining Chesapeake lighthouses represent less than half the number of light stations that graced the Bay in the early years of the twentieth century, but it is a fact—a fact that prompts two questions. First, why were there so many lighthouse stations on the Bay? And, second, when and why were they lost?

The history of Chesapeake Bay lights is somewhat at odds with the romantic conception of the tall, lonely tower on a dangerous outcropping, stoic above a foaming sea or of the isolated keeper who struggles against the elemental forces of nature. The story of the lighthouses and the lightkeepers of the Chesapeake Bay is not an exceptional tangent of American history, but part and parcel of it (and right at its political, economic and cultural center), beginning with the European settlement of a protected and bountiful estuary. It is the story of a people whose productive economy, transportation system, and social pleasures developed almost wholly around the Bay's waterways. And it is the story of the busy commerce that flourished in its small towns and cities, its many semi-rural communities, its growing metropolises (including the federal capital), and the lively exchange of its unusually cosmopolitan and well-traveled people.

The natural history of the Bay explains most of the navigational difficulties which, from colonial times, have been troublesome to ships. Briefly, the Chesapeake Bay, the drowned valley of the Susquehanna River, is the largest estuarine system in the United States. Created in the 15,000 years since the retreat of last glacier, the Chesapeake Bay is just under two hundred miles in length with a surface area of approximately 2,500 square miles—4,400 square miles if one includes the hundreds of creeks and rivers that make up the whole tidal system. The Bay's complex shoreline is over 8,000 miles, about equally divided between Maryland and Virginia.[1]

To get a picture of the Bay's substratum, one must retreat through geological time to imagine the young and mighty Susquehanna and the innumerable tributaries and streams whose waters flowed, from east and west, into the giant river. Slowly the Susquehanna excavated a deep valley that emptied into the ocean at what are now the Virginia Capes.[2] As the polar ice caps continued to melt, geological changes, especially the gradual sinking of the land, also contributed to the formation of the Bay. "The principal valley, in its lower course, eventually became so low that the sea engulfed its mouth. The subsidence continued gradually, and in time the sea thrust its flood tides halfway up the valley and into the lower portions of the valleys of the principal tributaries. At this point in the transition, the river was still a steadily-flowing stream of fresh water in its upper courses, but in its lower reaches it had become a salt-water estuary, accessible to the flux and reflux of the tides. ... Now the tides of the ocean, pushing their way two hundred miles inland, are stopped only by the great elevation of the adjacent

c. 1890, National Archives

No doubt the simplest of "lighthouses," this lantern at Goose Hill Channel, Virginia was lit by a light attendant. Light attendants were responsible for refueling lamps at regular intervals and were stationed at Light Attendant Stations (LAS) around the Bay. Many of these small stations became the Small Boat Stations of today's Coast Guard.

piedmont plateau. The beds of resistant deposits that formed the water sheds of the post-Pleistocene valleys, upon submergence became the long, interfluvial points of land—called 'necks'—so characteristic of the region today."[3]

It is worth noting that some of the earliest Chesapeake lighthouses were built on these necks, identifying the danger that the continuing hard ledge of the river's watershed posed to ships and the shallows that sedimentary deposits created.

Like most estuarine systems, much of the Chesapeake Bay's substratum is unsettled. Eddies and cross currents are created where fresh water, spilling down the Bay's innumerable tributaries (and lighter than water of high salinity), meets the rhythmical ebb and flow of the ocean tides. Much of the Chesapeake is relatively shallow, fed with the deposits of streams and rivers, and the mud and sand that is washed in by ocean waves, especially during storms. For almost four hundred years, the Bay and its tributaries have also been altered by the diversification and acceleration of human activity, beginning, in the seventeenth century, with the clearing of forested lands, increasing with industrialization and urbanization in the nineteenth century, and, finally, in the twentieth, with almost unbroken development, including the expansion and intensification of agricultural enterprise on both shores.

With no lighthouses and few good maps, a seventeenth or eighteenth century ship could not stand into the Bay in foul weather or at night, and, even in daylight,

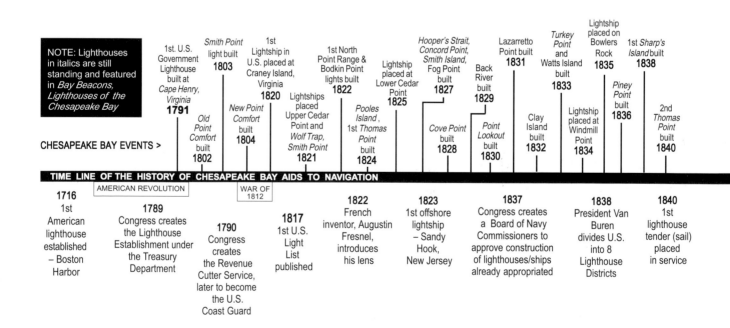

NOTE: Lighthouses in italics are still standing and featured in *Bay Beacons, Lighthouses of the Chesapeake Bay*

CHESAPEAKE BAY EVENTS >

1st. U.S. Government Lighthouse built at *Cape Henry, Virginia* **1791**

Old Point Comfort built **1802**

Smith Point light built **1803**

New Point Comfort built **1804**

1st Lightship in U.S. placed at Craney Island, Virginia **1820**

Lightships placed Upper Cedar Point and *Wolf Trap*, Smith Point **1821**

1st North Point Range & Bodkin Point lights built **1822**

Pooles Island, 1st *Thomas Point* built **1824**

Lightship placed at Lower Cedar Point **1825**

Hooper's Strait, Concord Point, Smith Island, Fog Point built **1827**

Cove Point built **1828**

Back River built **1829**

Point Lookout built **1830**

Lazarretto Point built **1831**

Clay Island built **1832**

Turkey Point and *Watts Island* built **1833**

Lightship placed at Windmill Point **1834**

Lightship placed on *Bowlers Rock* **1835**

Piney Point built **1836**

1st *Sharp's Island* built **1838**

2nd *Thomas Point* built **1840**

TIME LINE OF THE HISTORY OF CHESAPEAKE BAY AIDS TO NAVIGATION

AMERICAN REVOLUTION

WAR OF 1812

1716
1st American lighthouse established – Boston Harbor

1789
Congress creates the Lighthouse Establishment under the Treasury Department

1790
Congress creates the Revenue Cutter Service, later to become the U.S. Coast Guard

1817
1st U.S. Light List published

1822
French inventor, Augustin Fresnel, introduces his lens

1823
1st offshore lightship – Sandy Hook, New Jersey

1837
Congress creates a Board of Navy Commissioners to approve construction of lighthouses/ships already appropriated

1838
President Van Buren divides U.S. into 8 Lighthouse Districts

1840
1st lighthouse tender (sail) placed in service

2

often needed assistance to reach a good river channel. Pilots were a wise choice for ship's captains not thoroughly acquainted with the bottom of the Bay. In the early days of European settlement, the river channels were unobstructed and often quite deep—navigable for thirty, seventy, one hundred or more miles—for even the largest ships.

The beauty and bounty of the Chesapeake Bay astonished early explorers and colonists who found in its temperate loveliness and wealth of natural resources an irresistible invitation to enter and to stay. The variable forests and marshlands that fringed the Bay and its tributaries offered prosperity to diverse species of birds, fish, crabs, mollusks, and mammals of both sea and land,[4] —a veritable "zoological garden," as one newcomer enthusiastically wrote.

The great number of navigational aids placed on the Chesapeake Bay in the nineteenth century was a direct consequence of the busy and lucrative trade—local, regional and international—that, beginning in the seventeenth century, developed along its shores. The fur trade, the aggressive cutting of the majestic virgin forests, the tobacco plantation system and other farming all tended to favor the dispersement of the European population throughout the Tidewater region. As the English colonies of Maryland and Virginia prospered, the Chesapeake Bay's complex system of waterways made travel relatively easy—even enticing. Ferries, canoes, passenger sloops—indeed, every known kind of boat—carried people and their goods wherever they needed or wanted to go. There was little necessity for either towns or roads; below the fall lines, the creeks, rivers, and Bay admirably fulfilled all transportation needs—a dream come true in an age of ship-borne commerce. In fact, in the early years of the nineteenth century, the nation's very idea of future progress was the extension of uninterrupted river-borne commerce above the fall lines, into the Ohio Valley, to the Great Lakes and beyond—across the farthest western reaches of the continent.

With the exception of the Cape Henry light, which was not finished before the tide of revolution swept the colonies, the British failed to provide much-needed navigational aids on the Chesa-

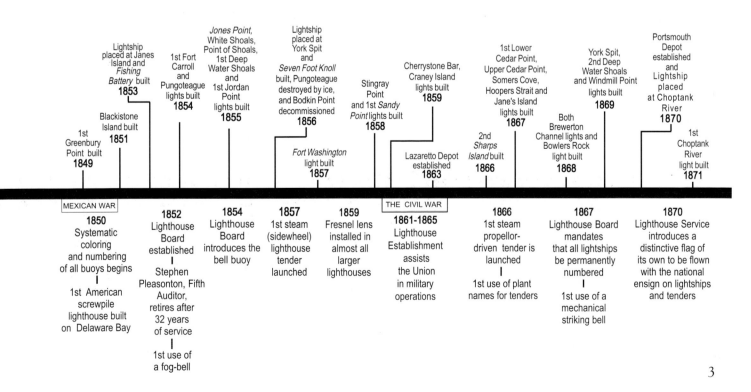

1st Greenbury Point built **1849**

Lightship placed at Janes Island and *Fishing Battery* built **1853**

Blackistone Island built **1851**

1st Fort Carroll and Pungoteague lights built **1854**

Jones Point, White Shoals, Point of Shoals, 1st Deep Water Shoals and 1st Jordan Point lights built **1855**

Lightship placed at York Spit and *Seven Foot Knoll* built, Pungoteague destroyed by ice, and Bodkin Point decommissioned **1856**

Fort Washington light built **1857**

Stingray Point and 1st *Sandy Point* lights built **1858**

Cherrystone Bar, Craney Island lights built **1859**

Lazaretto Depot established **1863**

1st Lower Cedar Point, Upper Cedar Point, Somers Cove, Hoopers Strait and Jane's Island lights built **1867**

2nd *Sharps Island* built **1866**

Both Brewerton Channel lights and Bowlers Rock light built **1868**

York Spit, 2nd Deep Water Shoals and Windmill Point lights built **1869**

Portsmouth Depot established and Lightship placed at Choptank River **1870**

1st Choptank River light built **1871**

MEXICAN WAR

1850 Systematic coloring and numbering of all buoys begins

1st American screwpile lighthouse built on Delaware Bay

1852 Lighthouse Board established

Stephen Pleasonton, Fifth Auditor, retires after 32 years of service

1st use of a fog-bell

1854 Lighthouse Board introduces the bell buoy

1857 1st steam (sidewheel) lighthouse tender launched

1859 Fresnel lens installed in almost all larger lighthouses

THE CIVIL WAR

1861-1865 Lighthouse Establishment assists the Union in military operations

1866 1st steam propellor-driven tender is launched

1st use of plant names for tenders

1867 Lighthouse Board mandates that all lightships be permanently numbered

1st use of a mechanical striking bell

1870 Lighthouse Service introduces a distinctive flag of its own to be flown with the national ensign on lightships and tenders

3

Light attendant duties included refueling lamps in strange locations such as the lamp inside a box, in a tree. Apparently in this photo, the lamp was removed for refueling. Lamps were usually filled at intervals of 5, 7 or 14 days—depending on the size of the lantern's reservoir.

peake Bay. The federal government of the United States lost no time in voicing its special intention to improve maritime security on the Bay—but, after an initial flurry of construction, funds proved scant and the British blockade of the Chesapeake during the War of 1812 occasioned a few steps backward.

Meanwhile, however, in the early 1800s, a Massachusetts ship's captain, Winslow Lewis (whose maritime career had been abruptly curtailed by Jefferson's trade embargo), had taken it upon himself to design a reflecting apparatus for lighthouses, to furnish construction plans and to invest the necessary energy to begin the building and outfitting of a modest lighthouse establishment. With the help of a respectable though glumly uninspired accountant who held the purse strings in the Treasury Department, and, on the Bay, a like-minded entrepreneur (John Donahoo of Havre de Grace), Lewis' initiative began to bear fruit. In the 1820s, lighthouse towers and rooftop lanterns began to dot likely points of land and well-placed islands throughout the Chesapeake Bay. By the mid-1820s, Winslow Lewis was, for all practical purposes, the unofficial commissioner of lighthouses: patentee of the reflecting apparatus then in use in all United States lighthouses, sole purchaser and supplier of whale oil, and exclusive contractor for light installations and repairs. Though there were, in this early period, a few superbly trained architectural engineers—such as Henry Latrobe—interested in the

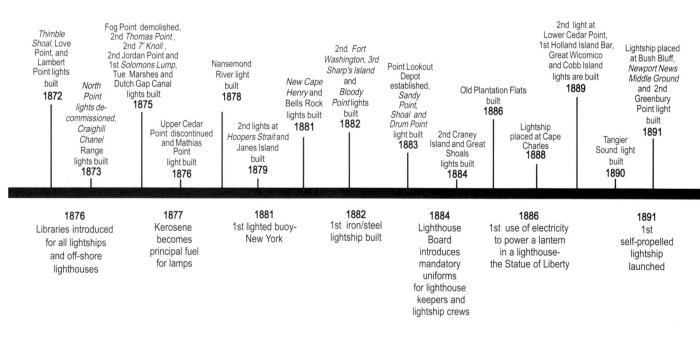

Thimble Shoal, Love Point, and Lambert Point lights built **1872**

North Point lights decommissioned, Craighill Chanel Range lights built **1873**

Fog Point demolished, 2nd *Thomas Point*, 2nd *7' Knoll* , 2nd Jordan Point and 1st *Solomons Lump*, Tue Marshes and Dutch Gap Canal lights built **1875**

Upper Cedar Point discontinued and Mathias Point light built **1876**

Nansemond River light built **1878**

2nd lights at *Hoopers Strait* and Janes Island built **1879**

New Cape Henry and Bells Rock lights built **1881**

2nd *Fort Washington, 3rd Sharp's Island* and *Bloody Point* lights built **1882**

Point Lookout Depot established, *Sandy Point, Shoal* and Drum Point light built **1883**

2nd *Craney* Island and Great Shoals lights built **1884**

Old Plantation Flats built **1886**

Lightship placed at Cape Charles **1888**

2nd light at Lower Cedar Point, 1st Holland Island Bar, Great Wicomico and Cobb Island lights are built **1889**

Tangier Sound light built **1890**

Lightship placed at Bush Bluff, *Newport News Middle Ground* and 2nd Greenbury Point light built **1891**

1876 Libraries introduced for all lightships and off-shore lighthouses

1877 Kerosene becomes principal fuel for lamps

1881 1st lighted buoy- New York

1882 1st iron/steel lightship built

1884 Lighthouse Board introduces mandatory uniforms for lighthouse keepers and lightship crews

1886 1st use of electricity to power a lantern in a lighthouse- the Statue of Liberty

1891 1st self-propelled lightship launched

country's maritime progress, and ready to submit bids on lighthouse construction, at this time in American society (perhaps, it can be said, as ever since) there had developed a distinct inclination to favor the self-made contractor and businessman.

During roughly the same time frame in Europe, improvements in the science of optics and the considerable ingenuity of one man, Augustin Fresnel, resulted in the design of a markedly superior illuminating apparatus—a hand-cut crystal lens whose prisms focused the light from a modest wick lamp into a brilliant horizontal sheet of light. Apparently, neither Lewis nor the Fifth Auditor of the Treasury took serious note of this vast improvement, preferring instead to keep to business as usual. But ships' captains, mariners and passengers observed the growing superiority of the French and British lights and complaints were soon forthcoming—complaints all the more vociferous because the keepers, lacking supervision and training, were held to no objective standards.

In the early years of the nineteenth century, lighthouse keeping tended to be a family occupation, involving children, wives and an assortment of other relatives (sometimes, too, slaves or hired help), and the tools employed—as well as the ideas about how to use them and how to keep a light—were as idiosyncratic as the keepers themselves. In fact, however, this apparently shoddy, make-do state of affairs—much maligned in retrospect—was almost certainly not unusual at this time in American history; it was, after all, a nation whose workforce was often constituted within the family group, whose tools were the private property (even the private manufacture) of those who used them. The predominant work ethic aimed at self-sufficiency and, in this still largely preindustrial economy, performance was self-regulated rather than mandated by wage contracts that specified a rigid routine or a repetitive and stylized performance of tasks.

Beginning in 1838, formal congressional inquiries responded to the growing number of complaints. Studies of both the United States and European lighthouse establishments were made by specially appointed investigative teams—on the whole, confirming the marked inferiority of American lighthouses and lightships. Besides becoming enamored of the French-cut lens, the investigators'

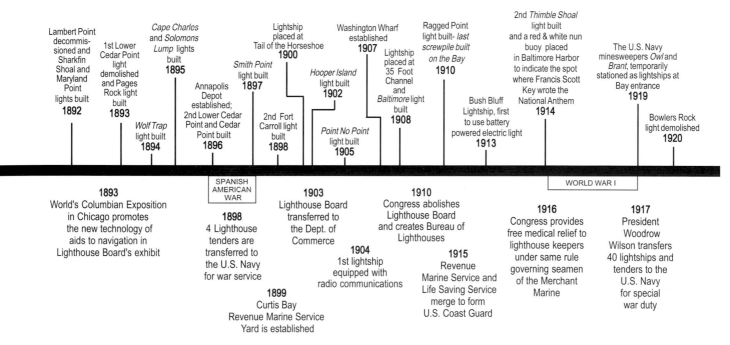

c.1912, National Archives

The light attendant of the post lantern at Randall Wharf on Back Creek off the Elk River, Maryland, had to row out to the middle of the river to refuel the lamp. His job could have been easier but the river repeatedly destroyed the long footbridge.

interest in a British engineer's newly designed, flanged lighthouse infrastructure was aroused—something that shortly proved significant for the Chesapeake Bay. By 1852, a new nine-member body of civilian and military experts had been constituted as the Lighthouse Board, modeling itself on the French lighthouse establishment. On the Chesapeake Bay, the old reflectors were soon replaced with sparkling Fresnel lenses and newly designed wick lamps, and, in the years immediately preceding and following the Civil War, many new screwpile lighthouses were built on heretofore inaccessible Chesapeake shoals.

Though the Chesapeake Bay was not a major theater of belligerent activity during the Civil War, its light stations were under almost constant surveillance by the Potomac Flotilla, and disconcerting skirmishes occurred with enough regularity to occasion considerable damage to lighthouse property. The Bay's lightships

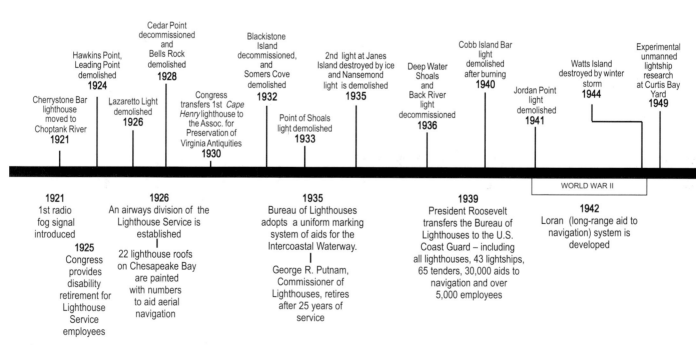

Cherrystone Bar lighthouse moved to Choptank River
1921

Hawkins Point, Leading Point demolished
1924

Lazaretto Light demolished
1926

Cedar Point decommissioned and Bells Rock demolished
1928

Congress transfers 1st *Cape Henry* lighthouse to the Assoc. for Preservation of Virginia Antiquities
1930

Blackistone Island decommissioned, and Somers Cove demolished
1932

Point of Shoals light demolished
1933

2nd light at Janes Island destroyed by ice and Nansemond light is demolished
1935

Deep Water Shoals and Back River light decommissioned
1936

Cobb Island Bar light demolished after burning
1940

Jordan Point light demolished
1941

Watts Island destroyed by winter storm
1944

Experimental unmanned lightship research at Curtis Bay Yard
1949

WORLD WAR II

1921
1st radio fog signal introduced

1925
Congress provides disability retirement for Lighthouse Service employees

1926
An airways division of the Lighthouse Service is established

1926
22 lighthouse roofs on Chesapeake Bay are painted with numbers to aid aerial navigation

1935
Bureau of Lighthouses adopts a uniform marking system of aids for the Intercoastal Waterway.

George R. Putnam, Commissioner of Lighthouses, retires after 25 years of service

1939
President Roosevelt transfers the Bureau of Lighthouses to the U.S. Coast Guard – including all lighthouses, 43 lightships, 65 tenders, 30,000 aids to navigation and over 5,000 employees

1942
Loran (long-range aid to navigation) system is developed

proved especially attractive guerilla targets and often disappeared deep into an inlet or river for several days. Two lightships were completely destroyed by the Confederates and several lighthouses were robbed of their supplies and vandalized or, occasionally, destroyed. Of great importance was the expansion and consolidation of the federal government that began during this period—first in Maryland, which was quite literally occupied by federal forces, and, following the war, at the Virginia Capes.

Beginning in 1852, the Lighthouse Board devoted its attention to the replacement of lights, to the provision of a uniform set of tools and to delivery of those supplies (now quality controlled) necessary to keep a good light. On the Chesapeake Bay, these years brought a golden age of lighthouse construction to a population whose lives—and livelihoods—still included a close intimacy with its waterways. Steamship lines, filled to capacity with passengers and goods, plied its waters; commerce of all kinds was brisk; fishing and the seasonal hunting of migratory waterfowl were astonishingly productive; industry—light and heavy—was growing and, along with it, major metropolitan areas, especially Baltimore. All of this activity was connected, up and down the entire length of the Bay. News traveled swiftly and had (as it had since colonial times) a global reach.

It is important to remember that the lighthouse establishment of the Chesapeake Bay included much more than the lighthouse stations proper. In the years before the Civil War, there were as many as nine lightships (including the country's first) on location throughout the Bay. Following the Civil War, though the number of lightships declined, the number of tenders and buoy depots began to increase, as did the number and type of buoys in use. The largest depots on the Bay (at Baltimore and Portsmouth) offered berthing and repair for lightships and tenders, functioned as receiving stations for every conceivable supply—including the iron work for enormous caisson structures and the iron piles used to anchor cottage lighthouses in the Bay. Additionally, they were often manufacturing centers, assembly workshops, and storage facilities—even research laboratories. Tenders with large crew complements steamed thousands of miles in their assigned regions annually—delivering coal, oil, food rations and other supplies, making repairs, hauling in buoys for maintenance, taking the inspectors out to

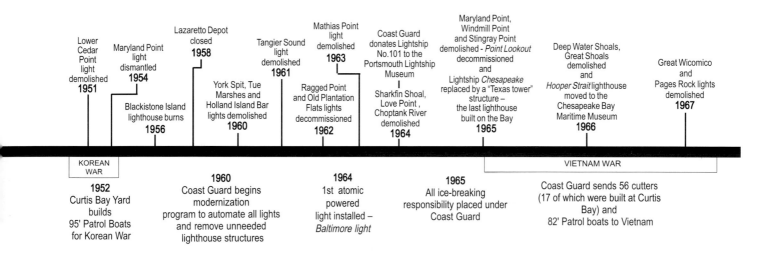

c. 1900, National Archives

The post lantern at Naval Hospital, Virginia, in Norfolk's harbor was maintained by a light attendant probably out of the Portsmouth Depot just across the river. The building at the end of the dock was a bath house for patients of the hospital and unrelated to the lantern.

lighthouse stations, towing lightships blown off station, and assisting in the many lighthouse construction projects on the Bay. Finally, the Bay had many post lights on its rivers whose daily upkeep and lighting required additional employees.

By the time of the Columbia Exposition of 1893, though the Bay continued to expand its lively lighthouse establishment, the Lighthouse Board had changed. For one thing, it was thoroughly bureaucratized, and there was more emphasis on formality and ceremony as well as on employee discipline and duty. For lightkeepers, job security was still poor and pay was stagnant—even after civil service status was granted to employees in 1896. Once again, the United States lighthouse establishment began to fall behind its European counterparts, this time in terms of personnel management rather than technological expertise.

In 1910 the Lighthouse Board was dissolved and aids to navigation were placed in the Department of Commerce where they remained until 1939. The Chesapeake

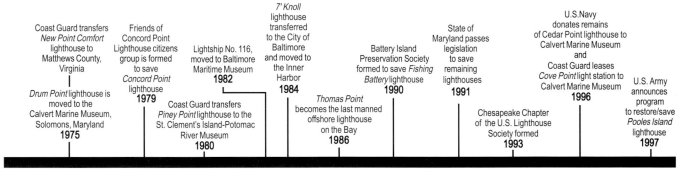

Coast Guard transfers *New Point Comfort* lighthouse to Matthews County, Virginia

Drum Point lighthouse is moved to the Calvert Marine Museum, Solomons, Maryland
1975

Friends of Concord Point Lighthouse citizens group is formed to save *Concord Point* lighthouse
1979

Coast Guard transfers *Piney Point* lighthouse to the St. Clement's Island-Potomac River Museum
1980

Lightship No. 116, moved to Baltimore Maritime Museum
1982

7' Knoll lighthouse transferred to the City of Baltimore and moved to the Inner Harbor
1984

Thomas Point becomes the last manned offshore lighthouse on the Bay
1986

Battery Island Preservation Society formed to save *Fishing Battery* lighthouse
1990

State of Maryland passes legislation to save remaining lighthouses
1991

Chesapeake Chapter of the U.S. Lighthouse Society formed
1993

U.S.Navy donates remains of Cedar Point lighthouse to Calvert Marine Museum and Coast Guard leases *Cove Point* light station to Calvert Marine Museum
1996

U.S. Army announces program to restore/save *Pooles Island* lighthouse
1997

1982
Coast Guard 5th District initiates "spruce-up" program for un-manned lighthouses

1984
Last U.S. lightship, the *Nantucket* is replaced by an automated navigation buoy.

U.S. Lighthouse Society in San Francisco, is formed

1995
Coast Guard 5th District refocuses maintenance program to balance work on navigational aids between private contractors and Coast Guard personnel

1996
Coast Guard 5th District releases statement of intent for future disposal/preservation of District's lighthouses

1st of a new class of buoy tenders named after lighthouse keepers is launched by Coast Guard

Bay lighthouses were not a major focus of Bureau of Lighthouse administration. The new Lighthouse Bureau put great emphasis on "economies in operation." On the Bay, there was essentially no new construction and repairs were often inadequate. At the same time, automation of Bay lights was begun in earnest. Though the Commissioner fought hard to obtain excellent benefits for his personnel, the expense of these benefits was offset by the withdrawal of keepers from lights that could be automated. During the 1920s and 1930s, the Chesapeake Bay lost lightkeepers at a considerably higher rate than the lighthouse establishment as a whole. Still, navigation was made safer during this period by the widespread use of radio communication and the installation of radio distance-finding stations.

The federal military stronghold on the Bay continued to increase well into the twentieth century, creating strange no-man's lands in what, for the most part, had been an uninterrupted web of interconnected communities. Following World War II, the technological superiority of the Army and Navy may have inadvertently promoted a devaluation of the Bay's quaint cottage lighthouses, especially after the lighthouse administration, including all its civilian employees, was relocated in the relatively small, underrated, underfunded and severely overburdened United States Coast Guard. More than anything, the unprecedented size, secrecy and power of Cold War military organization represented a radical departure from the traditional intimacies of life on the Bay and inevitably exerted a strong influence. The loss of the Chesapeake's lighthouses, however, began in the 1920s and cost-efficiency was the primary motive. Sometimes lights were decommissioned and torn down, but often they began to deteriorate after automation. Vandalism was difficult to control on the Chesapeake's accessible waterways. Public interest in lighthouse preservation was not high until many had disappeared.

In the exorbitant generosity of the early Chesapeake landscape and the experience of its early settlers, it is not difficult to find the familiar contours of some contemporary American values. First and foremost, perhaps, is the unabashed love of personal mobility—the dream of having fluid, easy transport, wherever one wants to go. Then, one may discern some interesting parallels between early settlement patterns and the contemporary enthusiasm for scattered development—a love of personal space that on the negative side of the ledger often gives way to disregard for the cultural value of cities. Inevitably, the story of the lost lighthouses of the Chesapeake Bay leads into the territory of national history, revealing aspects of its uniqueness, its triumphs, disappointments and sorry mistakes. How fortunate it is that behind this history the beauty and magic of the Chesapeake Bay still bid welcome.

The post lantern at Sand Shoal Inlet, Virginia. During the day, the four slats of colored wood acted as a day marker. Hundreds of such hand-fueled lamps once dotted the shallow waters of the Bay.

National Archives

9

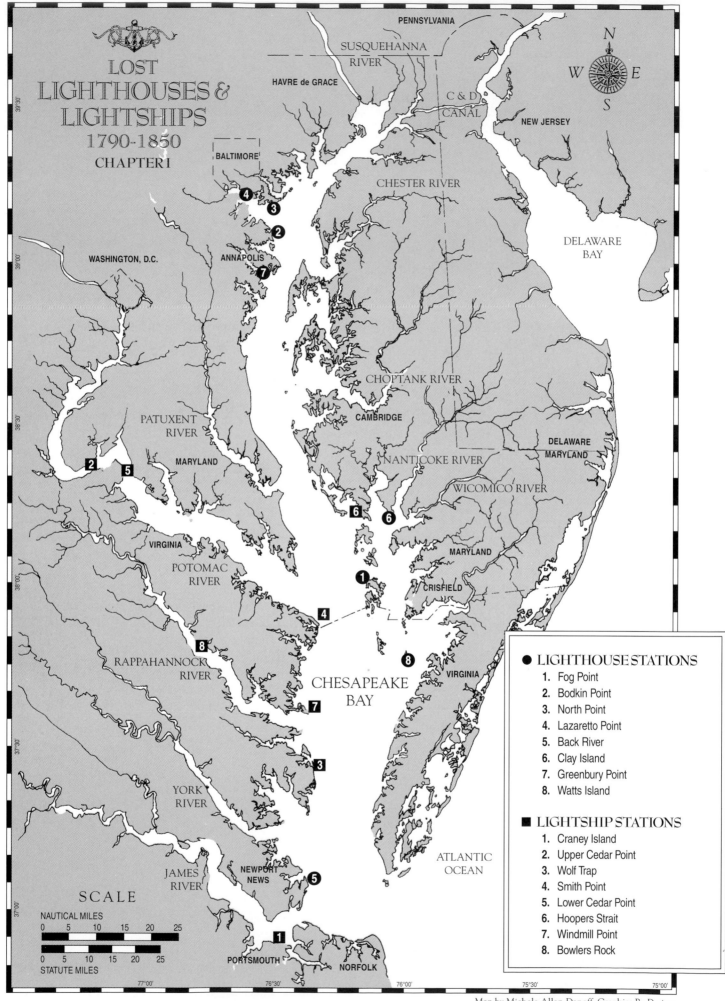

LOST LIGHTHOUSES & LIGHTSHIPS
1790-1850
CHAPTER I

PENNSYLVANIA

SUSQUEHANNA RIVER

HAVRE de GRACE

C & D CANAL

NEW JERSEY

BALTIMORE

CHESTER RIVER

DELAWARE BAY

WASHINGTON, D.C.

ANNAPOLIS

CHOPTANK RIVER

PATUXENT RIVER

CAMBRIDGE

MARYLAND

DELAWARE
MARYLAND

NANTICOKE RIVER

WICOMICO RIVER

VIRGINIA

MARYLAND

POTOMAC RIVER

CRISFIELD

RAPPAHANNOCK RIVER

CHESAPEAKE BAY

VIRGINIA

YORK RIVER

ATLANTIC OCEAN

JAMES RIVER

NEWPORT NEWS

SCALE

NAUTICAL MILES
0   5   10   15   20   25

0   5   10   15   20   25
STATUTE MILES

PORTSMOUTH   NORFOLK

● LIGHTHOUSE STATIONS
1. Fog Point
2. Bodkin Point
3. North Point
4. Lazaretto Point
5. Back River
6. Clay Island
7. Greenbury Point
8. Watts Island

■ LIGHTSHIP STATIONS
1. Craney Island
2. Upper Cedar Point
3. Wolf Trap
4. Smith Point
5. Lower Cedar Point
6. Hoopers Strait
7. Windmill Point
8. Bowlers Rock

39°30'
39°00'
38°30'
38°00'
37°30'
37°00'

77°00'   76°30'   76°00'   75°30'   75°00'

Map by Michele Allan Danoff, Graphics By Design.

CHAPTER I

At the beginning of the nineteenth century, the Chesapeake region remained remarkably rural, and the city of Washington, with the grand design of its unpaved avenues slashed through forest and field, was dubiously regarded by many—a city of streets without buildings, observers noted wryly, to be distinguished from neighboring Georgetown, a city of buildings without streets.[1]

Even so, the region was also unusually cosmopolitan—its people blessed with the extraordinary mobility that the navigability of the Bay and its many tributaries had long afforded, and enriched by the vast oceanic trade upon which the colonies of Maryland and Virginia had been built. Sloops, schooners and passenger packets sped across its waters, from Alexandria and Georgetown, to Annapolis, Baltimore and Havre de Grace, south to Norfolk and up the James to Richmond, and farther still, to Liverpool and London, to name but a few ports of call, laden with passengers, livestock, and every kind of commodity.

As seen by the population of the early 1800s, development was in no small part dependent on the improvement of waterways: for the Chesapeake and the rivers below the fall lines, by the placement of lighthouses and buoys that would render commercial and passenger traffic on the Bay faster, safer and more profitable; for the Piedmont and mountainous regions to the west, canals that would bear boats and barges around rocky outcroppings and carry them above the fall lines; canals that would bring the coal, pig iron, wheat, timber and manufactured items back to the towns and growing cities of the Tidewater.

In 1789, the First Congress of the United States enacted legislation placing aids to navigation under federal control and urged timely completion of the unfinished Cape Henry light. This work proceeded smoothly and followed closely the engineering and architectural plans that the British had drawn up, though in the intervening years of the Revolution, most of the original stone had been buried in the shifting sands of the windy cape. The quarrying of new stone at Aquia Creek on the Potomac River quickly drew attention to the need for more effective navigational aids on the Bay, for the stone was loaded onto sailing barges that too often grounded as they entered the Bay at Smith Point. "Only through Herculean efforts were these stone-carrying ships freed from Smith Point's hard sand bottom. Skippers of these same vessels demanded that Congress install a buoy for their navigational guidance."[2]

Agitation by ships' captains and merchants for navigational aids in the waters of the Chesapeake Bay was, of course, not new, and as such aids were established, their maintenance and security became a matter of grave concern. In 1794, for example, Virginia's state assembly passed an act making the removal, sinking or destruction of a buoy a felony punishable "by death without benefit of clergy."[3]

In many ways, what is most notable about early U.S. lighthouse administration is the swiftness and eagerness with which federal legislation establishing jurisdiction over lighthouses and floating aids was promulgated. Clearly, it was a government whose continued independence, in the eyes of its elected officials, demanded close attention to all that favored successful maritime commerce. Nevertheless, the need to establish a system of reliable maritime aids was not easily translated into effective action. Government funds were scant and there were many other demands to

Between 1820 and 1852, the U.S. lighthouse establishment grew seven-fold, but administration proceedures and technology remained stagnant.

11

Stephen Pleasonton, Fifth Auditor, Department of the Treasury, 1820 to 1852. Pleasonton is the favorite villain of lighthouse historians. Indeed, his photograph suggests a man of singular character, if not exactly charm.

be met by the emergent federal entity. For this reason, it seems all the more remarkable that three fairly distinguished Chesapeake Bay towers were completed by 1804 and that all were so well built that they are still standing (Old Cape Henry, 1791, Old Point Comfort, 1802, and New Point Comfort, 1804). During the first thirty-five years of lighthouse administration, the number of lighthouses increased from ten to fifty-five—each "built to meet immediate and pressing local want, and without reference to any general system"[4]—but on the Chesapeake Bay almost twenty years passed before a second period of construction brought many still-familiar lights to the Tidewater. For a time at least, the threat of war with England tended to dampen enthusiasm for placement of navigational aids on the Bay. During the War of 1812, buoys were deliberately removed in the hope that British warships would run aground. For example, "[w]hen the British entered the Potomac in 1813 on their way to the nation's capital, the Smith Point Light was extinguished and the buoy removed by orders of the Federal government."[5] In all, there were twenty-three groundings of British ships.

With the end of hostilities, the Potomac ports quickly regained their commercial importance and, in consort with other growing Chesapeake Bay metropolises, especially Baltimore, demands for the placement of reliable navigational aids were vigorously renewed. Thus, it might be said that the principal story of the Bay's beacons begins with the lighthouses and lightships built in the 1820s. At this time, the lighthouse establishment was placed under the direction of the Fifth Auditor of the Department of Treasury, Stephen Pleasonton—the latest in a series of moves designed to free the president and his cabinet from the day-to-day supervision of the lighthouses and their keepers.[6]

Among lighthouse historians, it is habitual to point a disapproving finger at Stephen Pleasonton, a notorious bean counter whose overall lack of understanding of maritime matters was matched only by his ignorance of both ship and lighthouse construction. His unpopularity probably originated in the tone of condescension and exasperation that infected so much of his correspondence with the Investigating Committee of the Lighthouse Board in 1851, a tone which, not incidentally, led to his vilification in its published report to Congress. It is quite possibly rare in the history of government bureaucracy for a single individual of sound mind and responsible principles to suffer such resounding criticism, and thus it is perhaps worth examining why he has been so universally condemned.

First of all, Pleasonton, "did not have a professional organization under his direction. Actually, he and his staff in Washington were clerical administrators contracting for everything needed to maintain aids to navigation."[7] Second, it is probably fair to say that Pleasonton was not responsive to the impetus among the growing group of engineering and architectural professionals of the early 1800s "to transform the American lighthouse from its more mundane beginnings on this continent to more grandiose civic monuments after the European model."[8] Interestingly, it is known that one member of this group, engineer and architect Benjamin Henry Latrobe, submitted drawings for the North Point lighthouses shortly before he died in 1820. Last but not least, however, was Pleasonton's unpopularity with ships' masters. By them he was adjudged indifferent to the safety of ships and the lives of seamen—a complaint that probably cannot be assuaged by the passage of time.

Pleasonton was a number-cruncher and a bottom-liner of a sort, well known to contemporary folks, but meddlesome he was not. Under the superintendency of Pleasonton, lighthouse personnel were almost completely free of supervision and interference (working conditions that have not entirely lost their appeal, and, more importantly, working conditions that tell us much about attitudes toward discipline and the social temperament of the early United States). In short, Pleasonton's administrative style was *laissez-faire*, certainly an anathema to the military men and scientists who investigated the early lighthouse establishment and who, later, made up the governing body of the Lighthouse Board.

Invariably, Pleasonton's contracts were awarded to the lowest bidder—sometimes to contractors who had already proven themselves incapable of delivering quality construction (as happened at Bodkin Point and North Point). But, with the help of two or three reliable cronies and building contractors—most notably, Winslow Lewis, patentee of the parabolic reflector then in use in all U.S. lighthouses, and his business associate, John Donahoo of Havre de Grace, Maryland[9]—Pleasonton did succeed in dotting the Chesapeake shores with lighthouses of unassuming design and modest construction.

Of the lighthouses built on the Chesapeake Bay in the 1820s, more than half have disappeared—often the result of the Bay's excavation of the narrow necks of land extending into its waters. Where steps could be taken to protect such lighthouse stations from encroachment by the Bay, and where such steps were taken, the longevity of these stubby towers is testimony to their solid construction.

John Donahoo, a native of Havre de Grace and, for the better part of twenty years, an elected official of that community (first as judge of elections, later as town commissioner), was involved in the construction of as many as fifteen of the Chesapeake Bay's lighthouses. The records indicate that Donahoo consistently came in with the lowest bid on the lighthouse projects that he was awarded. Those that escaped his grasp generally went to Winslow Lewis—with the exception of the North Point and Bodkin Point lights. Here the builders proved so unsatisfactory that Donahoo was called in to shore up the structures. For example, records of the

city council in Havre de Grace show that Donahoo resigned to work on the North Point Lighthouse on November 30, 1830.[10] "[I]f he proved himself a competent and cost-efficient builder, his continued selection would no doubt be the logical path of least resistance."[11]

Winslow Lewis, especially his marked influence with Stephen Pleasonton, is often mentioned by lighthouse historians but rarely treated with any detail. Thus, he remains something of an enigma in the history of Chesapeake Bay lighthouses, and, more generally, in the history of the U.S. lighthouse establishment. Born on Cape Cod in 1770, the grandson of a highly educated, celebrated preacher, Winslow Lewis successfully followed his father and brothers into the profession of ship's captain, commanding transatlantic ships from 1796 to 1808 and becoming a member of the prestigious Boston Marine Society in 1797. When the 1807 Jefferson trade embargo brought his promising maritime career to an abrupt halt, Lewis—by then married and the father of six—showed unusual entrepreneurial skill, taking it upon himself "to use his mind to improve something susceptible of considerable improvement—something whose inefficacy he had noticed in his seafaring days—something euphemistically called 'The United States Light House Establishment.'"[12] Unlike the oft-repeated invective regarding the undistinguished career of Stephen Pleasonton, whose inaction has perhaps been given too much weight in the history of early lighthouse administration, the career of Winslow Lewis, whose ambition and inven-

Library of Congress

Winslow Lewis, lighthouse entrepreneur, 1770-1850

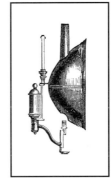

Lewis's parabolic reflector, patented in 1810, was similar to the lighting system developed by the Swiss inventor Argand in 1784. Lewis modified Argand's system by placing a convex lens in front of the lamp.

13

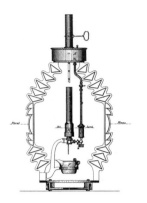

The principle of August Fresnel's lens was to surround the lamp with a ring of optic glass, with the prisms angled in such a way as to concentrate the lamp's light and magnify the power of the lamp inside. His lens and the single-wick lamp quickly replaced the inefficient multiple reflectors previously used. Although the type of lamp and fuel used changed numerous times over the years, the Fresnel lens remained the primary lighthouse illumination system throughout the world for over 100 years.

There are 6 classes of Fresnel lenses, from the largest 1st-class seacoast lens, 10' tall, to the smallest 6th-order lens, about 18" high. (A 3 1/2-order lens was later introduced.) Other than the lights at the entrance of the Bay, Fresnel lenses used on the Chesapeake were 4th, 5th or 6th- order lenses, as shown above, with a range of up to 12 miles. Examples of Fresnel lenses may be seen at almost all of the maritime museums in the Chesapeake Bay area.

tiveness were responsible for the organization of the service that Pleasonton took over as auditor, has been too much overlooked.[13]

Because Lewis's parabolic reflector was rendered obsolete by the Fresnel lens in the 1820s, it is sometimes forgotten that in the first decade of the nineteenth century, the science of optics was primitive, and had, as yet, no application to lighthouse illumination. "The illuminating apparatus ... commonly used in American lighthouses at this time was the so-called 'spider lamp,' merely a shallow container of whale oil with a number of wicks floating in it. Although this lamp perhaps surpassed the illumination provided by the 'twenty-four miserable candles' that illuminated the famous Eddystone Lighthouse until 1811, its superiority could not have been spectacular."[14]

Thus, Lewis turned his attention to the problems of illumination — obtaining a patent, in 1808, for a light designed for the binnacle of ships (patent No. 891) and, again, two years later, receiving a patent for his 'reflecting and magnifying lantern' (patent No. 1305). Lewis's Boston Marine Society connections were important and he used them well by arranging public exhibitions of his light in the Boston State House and the Boston lighthouse and inviting the society's members to compare the effectiveness of his light, which they did, writing a highly favorable report. Lewis lost no time. By July, an exhibition of the Lewis lights in

one of the twin lighthouses on Thatcher's Island had convinced the Boston collector of customs that all U.S. lighthouses should be equipped with Lewis's patent lamps—and he wrote as much to Secretary of the Treasury Albert Gallatin. Gallatin now urged Congress to allow government purchase of the patent right and to give Lewis a seven-year contract for "fitting up and keeping in repair, any or all of the lighthouses in the United States or the territories thereof." In return, Lewis "had to guarantee that his lights would be more brilliant than their predecessors and that they would save one- half of the quantity of oil previously consumed."[15]

For Lewis, however, this was only the beginning of his initiative. Soon he had convinced the government to purchase and refit a ninety-ton schooner, the *Federal Jack*, with "a blacksmith shop, a carpenter shop and accommodations for thirteen men," as well as to furnish all necessary equipment and two lightweight boats to transport the workmen and apparatus to the lighthouse sites. Lewis energetically went to work to fulfill his contract obligations, and, by the end of 1812, had already outfitted forty lighthouses. In March of 1813, however, the *Federal Jack* was captured by the British, and Lewis, his captain and men were arrested. Though he and his men were soon paroled, the *Federal Jack* was stripped and burned. Lewis was unable to complete his lighthouse contract until 1815, but his determined anti-British sentiment found expression in a variety of enterprises, including privateering.[16]

After the war, Lewis profitably diversified his interests into politics, rope-making, and textile manufacture. But he did not abandon his lighthouse activities and, by 1816, he had successfully negotiated a new government contract to supply the light stations with sperm oil (an unusually lucrative business, it turned out), to visit each light station annually to make any necessary repairs, and to report to the Department of Treasury on the condition of each station. "In effect, the contract made Winslow Lewis the *de facto* superintendent of lighthouses," an authority that he demonstrated quite directly the following year with publication of the first U.S. light list, a sixteen-page book entitled *Description of the Light Houses*.[17]

By now, the warp of the early lighthouse establishment taken over by Pleasonton in 1820 had been laid: A schooner with a nine-man crew traveled U.S. waters making once-a-year oil deliveries, checking the condition of the lights, and making repairs as needed. But Lewis was not finished. In 1818, the indomitable entrepreneur ventured into lighthouse construction, boldly assuming responsibility for a Latrobe-designed lighthouse on the Mississippi River that other contractors wouldn't touch—a design so complicated that even Lewis noted that the plan was "injudicious." In fact, two days before the structure was to have been completed, the whole building collapsed. Typically, Lewis emerged Phoenix-like from the ashes, using the building's collapse as the opportunity to submit his own plans, prudently specifying reuse of salvageable material from the original structure. He won the bid, satisfactorily completed the tower (at a little over one-tenth the cost of the Latrobe lighthouse), and, according to his estimate, went on to build approximately eighty more lighthouses.[18]

It is widely believed that Lewis was responsible for the design of many Chesapeake Bay lighthouses. "The early keeper's houses of the Chesapeake, as well as other parts of the country, are similar both in appearance and dimension . . . [leading] to the notion that a prototype was also used for these buildings"—something that is entirely in keeping with Pleasonton's administrative style.[19] It is known, for example, that Lewis devised "a set of plans for five different sizes of towers that he believed would meet the needs of any land locations," and that he built towers on several marine sites—structures that were the first of their kind and that presented formidable engineering challenges.[20]

But, if Winslow Lewis was the author of the early lighthouse building plans, Pleasonton, in later years, was not quite ready to admit it. Interrogated at length by the Investigating Committee of the Lighthouse Board, his written responses reveal the com-

Designed by Winslow Lewis, early Bay lighthouses such as Greenbury Point, Blackistone Island, Fishing Battery and Clay Island, may have been the prototypes for numerous other American lighthouses. A similar design can be seen in The Point Loma and Point Pinos, California lighthouses built in the mid-1800s. Indeed, the original lighthouse at Alcatraz Island and the first 7 Pacific coast lighthouses were built by contractors from Baltimore, Maryland.

Greenbury Point

bination of self-righteousness, evasiveness, and befuddlement, which so infuriated the Investigative Committee. "There is not," Pleasonton explained, "what may be called any general system of construction, though there are generally adopted . . . sizes of towers: [E]ach locality has had a particular plan and specification made for it."[21]

Anyway, Pleasonton avowed, the building plans would be difficult to come by: "To give the modes or plans employed, would involve sending copies of the contracts, specifications, and working-drawings of over three hundred light-houses; a labor which it is entirely out of my power to perform with the means of my office. Most of the specifications and working drawings were used up by the workmen... To give copies of these frivialities [*sic*] would be impossible, and useless if possible.[22]

Finally, Pleasonton's astonishing response regarding structural repairs to the lighthouse stations reveals the off-handed arrogance of a man who has never put saw to wood or hammer to nail. "As many different means are employed to restore impaired foundations," Pleasonton observed, "as there are foundations so impaired . . . The board will perceive the absurdity of requiring general answers to cases which vary with every variation of locality, and that, . . . [involve] nothing greater than the particular plan of shoring up a house, or underpinning a tower, in which all that is required is a small knowledge of ordinary mechanical means, such as is in the possession of every master-workman or engineer."[23]

What, one might well ask, were the characteristics of the Bay's first light-

15

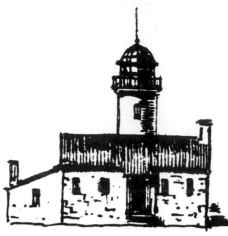

FOG POINT 1827-1875 The lighthouse at Fog Point was located at the northwestern edge of Smith Island. It was a stone tower-on-roof style house built by John Donahoo in 1827. The efficiency of the light at Fog Point was questionable and constant shoaling at the water's edge forced ships beyond the light's effective range. The Board recommended the decommissioning of the lighthouse, and in 1875, a new lighthouse was built at nearby Solomons Lump and Fog Point light was discontinued.

Sketches of Fog Point lighthouse found on site plans indicate the structure was similar to other "tower-on-house" lighthouses on the Bay, such as nearby Clay Island. The 1843 drawing (above) reflects the description of the house found in the Board's records. The saltbox roofline (opposite) on another 1843 drawing is an unproven design.

National Archives drawings

The Parson of the Islands, Rev. Joshua Thomas preached Methodism on, Deal, Smith, Tangier and Watt's Islands during the mid-1800s. Sailing between the islands in his canoe, the "Methodist", he sometimes stayed overnight at the lighthouses, for lack of hotel rooms on the islands. Collection P. Hornberger

houses? First and foremost, the early lighthouses were, of necessity, built on islands or points of land and were intended to mark extensive shoals dangerous to ships of deep draft. As such, they provided additional navigational assistance, most especially to the nighttime mariner, but were of more limited usefulness during squalls and northwesters, and almost certainly of no maritime assistance in severe storms or in heavy fog when the poor quality of the early nineteenth century illuminating apparatus and the land-based lantern's necessary distance from main shipping channels almost certainly meant that the light was invisible, the fog bell inaudible.

Most of these lighthouses were masonry or stone towers in the shape of truncated cones, approximately thirty feet in height, with a base diameter of eighteen to twenty feet that decreased to a diameter of nine or ten feet at the top, their thick walls giving them a sturdy gnome-like appearance. The tower supported a lantern deck with a radially laid stone or cast-iron floor, cantilevered beyond the top of the tower, and a catwalk with a cast-iron balustrade. The heavy cast-iron lantern was supported by masonry walls and the lantern set with triangular or rectangular glazed panels of approximately ten by twelve inches.

The keeper's humble one-and-a-half story dwelling, generally twenty by thirty-four feet, was separate—usually only a short distance from the tower—and followed a rigid floor plan, offering a small living room and one or two bedrooms with an attached kitchen and, sometimes, an unpretentious porch—a household arrangement that probably fairly reflects the modest expectations of many an early nineteenth century American family.

Of special note is the economical rooftop lantern, which, it has been said, was Pleasonton's favorite lighthouse structure. Several were built on the Chesapeake Bay, including the lights on Clay Island, Point Lookout, Greenbury Point and Fog Point. Those built at Jones Point, and—the last lighthouse built by John Donahoo—on Fishing

16

Continued on page 19

c. 1910, Maryland Historical Society

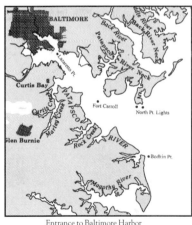

Entrance to Baltimore Harbor

BODKIN POINT 1822-1856 The lighthouse at Bodkin Point at the entrance to Baltimore was Maryland's first lighthouse. It was built by the Baltimore partners, Evans and Coppeck (who went on to build the eastern tower of the North Point Range) for $4,600. The 35' stone tower was placed next to a 20'x34' stone keeper's house. Winslow Lewis supplied the lighting apparatus. When the improved light at Seven Foot Knoll was built in 1856, the station was discontinued, left vacant for years, and finally destroyed in 1914. Until its destruction the old lighthouse was a popular local attraction and hide-away for lovers. The small island on which the lighthouse stood has disappeared.

The story is told that a fisherman living in the old keeper's house wanted to get married. When the preacher arrived, no boat was available to carry him across the narrow spit of water to the lighthouse. Undaunted, the preacher shouted the required vows across the water. The couple honeymooned on the Island.

NORTH POINT RANGE 1822-1873 Built just after Bodkin Point lighthouse, the two lights of the North Point Range were constructed on the north side of the entrance to the Patapsco River as an aid to ships entering Baltimore harbor. The towers were similar to others built during the administration of the Fifth Auditor. Both were of stone masonry. The eastern light (lower) stood in 3' of water, connected to shore by a 200' footbridge. The western tower (upper) stood in 5' of water, 700 yards from the eastern light, and 100 yards from the shore. The keeper, who tended both lights, lived in the 20'x34' stone dwelling on shore. He was paid almost double the annual wages for tending both lights.

There was more than a hint of local politics involved in the appointment of the first North Point keeper who, as a member of the Maryland House of Delegates, took annual leave in order to attend the General Assembly session in Annapolis. Complaints regarding the light's poor visibility were common and the value of their location frequently questioned. When the Craighill Channel Range lights were built in 1873, the North Point Range was decommissioned and left to deteriorate.

Mariners Museum

Coast Guard

BACK RIVER 1829-1936 A familiar landmark for over 125 years, the bayside station was situated on the south side of the entrance to Virginia's Back River and was built by Winslow Lewis for $3,500 (plus $750 for his lamps). At the request of the first keeper, William Jett, Lewis also added a porch to the house for an additional $15. The keeper's house was located 144' inland and a footbridge was needed to span the marsh out to the tower. Back River was sacked and ruined by Confederates in 1862, but it was the Bay's wave and wind that most threatened the light station. Riprap was repeatedly placed around the tower during the late 1800s, and blowing sand was such a nuisance that, at one point, screens were strategically placed around the station—with little effect. Like the 30'-tower, the detached dwelling was painted white. The photos of the dwelling shown here predate the 2nd-story addition to the keeper's house completed in 1894. A severe storm hit the station in October, 1903,when 14' waves dashed against the tower and dwelling. Repaired again, the station's days were numbered and, after automation, it remained untended until 1936 when it was decommissioned. The final days came in 1956, when *Hurricane Flossie* completely destroyed the remaining buildings.

Coast Guard

This romantacized postcard shows the rubble-protected shore of Back River light. *c. 1920*

Collection of Richard Julian

Battery in the Susquehanna Flats near Havre de Grace, came after Pleasonton's time but followed closely the design of earlier stations. (The 1896 Cedar Point lighthouse, however, represented a much later design.) Although the Spartan dimensions of the early abodes are the same as those for a separate keeper's dwelling, the living space was certainly much more cramped because of the stairway to the lantern on the roof. Most of these dwellings were enlarged in the last decades of the nineteenth century.

It is almost certain that the uniformity of lighthouse design on the Chesapeake Bay has much to do with comfortable contractual arrangements between Donahoo, Lewis and Pleasonton—an association of long duration and measured achievement, but one that finally set the whole lighthouse establishment on a course of mediocrity, which was not entirely overcome until the next century. "Lost were the opportunities to create dramatic civic monuments in the European tradition or to develop more exotic structural forms to compensate for difficult coastline conditions. It also had its advantages. Gained was a thoroughly economic system for the rapid deployment of these navigational aids up and down the American coastline."[24]

The illuminating apparatus that Winslow Lewis sold to the United States in 1812 had three parts: a lamp, a reflector and a magnifier. The lamp, similar to Argand's fountain lamp, used a three-quarter-inch wick and was mounted on a circular iron frame in front of the reflector. The parabolic reflector was made of a thin sheet of silver-plated copper, and the magnifier—the *coup de grace* of this optic device—was a "so-called lens, of bottle-green glass, shaped like the bull's-eye let into ship's decks," about two-and-a-half inches thick and six inches in diameter. As it turned out, the light was faulty in both concept and design, and when its ambiguous optics were combined with careless manufacture—to wit, the thinness of the copper, which caused the reflector to bend with the slightest pressure (for example, in cleaning), the thinness, too, of the silver-plat-

ing, which instead of creating a bright reflection had the "grain and luster of tinware and would reflect no distant image," and, finally, the thick obscurity of the green glass—when all of this was enclosed by the tower's massive lantern, the effect, as one inspector later noted, was one of "making a bad light worse."[25] Nevertheless, the character of Lewis's parabolic reflector represented a notable improvement over previous lights and a tremendous economic gain in oil saved. Eventually, the paraboloid and its silver-plating were improved, but by 1840 the obscure green "magnifying glass" had been retired. Years later, the Lighthouse Board summed up the problems of Lewis's illuminating apparatus. When the reflectors were well-made, well-placed and in the hands of competent keepers, the Board conceded that a good light was possible—but their true feelings are probably better represented in the following statement: "War was made on the system of reflectors, and when the Light-House Establishment was turned over to the Light-House Board in 1852 the reflectors were replaced by the Fresnel lenticular apparatus . . . Its adoption in this country made it possible for a light-keeper of average capacity to keep a good light, and impossible for him to keep a bad one."[26]

Though certainly unintended, a system of local political patronage was easily effected in the selection of lighthouse keepers during Pleasonton's tenure as Fifth Auditor—and for at least twenty years before that—for the keepers were chosen and virtually appointed by the local revenue collector upon whom responsibility for local lighthouse administration had devolved. Thus, it is not surprising that the early lighthouse keepers varied widely, not only in occupational skill and in their understanding of maritime matters, but also in their overall dedication to the job. "Although keepers are pictured as belonging to an almost heroic breed," one local historian has remarked, ". . . many of the keepers looked upon their jobs as sinecures on which not a great deal of energy need be spent."[27]

The shortcomings of this system were surely compounded by a complete lack of training and by an almost total lack of re-

Continued on page 21

Adoption of the Fresnel lens "made it possible for a lightkeeper of average capacity to keep a good light, and impossible for him to keep a bad one."

19

LAZARETTO POINT 1831-1926 The light station at Lazaretto Point contained a fog bell, simple keeper's house and a solid seawall, but in this c.1868 photo, the station had not yet seen the industrial development of the Canton region nearby. The building with the Palladian window in the background is Baltimore City's "fever house" for smallpox, cholera, and yellow fever victims. In 1863, the building was acquired as part of the Lazaretto property expansion into a lighthouse depot. Industrial development and smoke stacks soon filled the skyline, crowding the light to the point that it was almost hidden by buildings. Behind the station, the lights of the nearby mills later confused navigators heading into the busy Port of Baltimore.

The 31' tower at Lazaretto was built by Donahoo in 1831. The stone tower was torn down and the light replaced by a simple steel skeletal tower in 1926. It stood until 1954, long after the station was discontinued. Fort McHenry can be seen in the background across the Patapsco River.

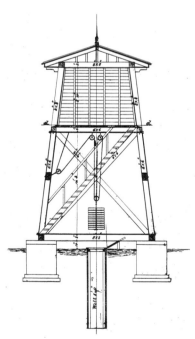

This 1886 design for the Lazaretto fog-bell tower shows the 8' well and the block-and-tackle system of weights (similar to the movement of a case clock) that automatically rang the fog bell.

sources—informational or material—that the keeper could tap into for improvement of the lighthouse station. Many responsible lighthouse keepers never saw an inspector and had no standard by which to judge the adequacy of their light, much less the means to improve it—even if they knew what needed to be done and how to accomplish it. Others probably didn't care. Some of the latter group procured unskilled laborers and slaves to fulfill their obligations as keepers. At some point, Pleasonton had a single page of instructions printed up and this was to be given to newly appointed lighthouse personnel—though many apparently later told investigators that they had never seen it.

In one area, however, especially by contemporary standards of social equality, the early lighthouse establishment was superior to subsequent lighthouse administration—and this was in the hiring of women. "So necessary is it," Pleasonton wrote, indirectly affirming the importance of women in maintaining lighthouse stations, "that the lights should be in the hands of experienced keepers, that I have, in order to effect that object as far as possible, recommended, on the death of a keeper, that his widow, if steady and respectable, should be appointed to succeed him . . ."[28] The first women keepers appeared in the 1830s. By 1851, there were, thirty women keepers—all widows of keepers who had died in service. But a scant decade later—though the number of light stations continued to expand (and, presumably, too, the number of widows), that number had shrunk to only fifteen. For example, the Potomac lights had many women keepers until Lighthouse Board regulations greatly diminished their number in the years following the Civil War. Josephine Freeman was recorded as keeper at Blackistone Island for over thirty-five years. Charlotte Suter tended Piney Point Light for several years before being fired for spending too much time at her tavern near the lighthouse. Altogether, Piney Point had four women keepers, two during Pleasonton's tenure: Charlotte Suter, 1844-1846, and Susan Nuthall, 1850-1861. Ann Davis kept Point Lookout light from 1830-1847.[29]

Mariners' Musuem, Ralph Smith Collection

A young woman attendant carries the lamp to a post lantern for the evening illumination, c.1925. We cannot be certain that she was a lighthouse service employee, for women were not required to wear uniforms.

Lightships—"the most picturesque, the most exposed, and the most isolated" of maritime beacons— are often treated as a discreet and even somewhat peripheral category of aids to navigation.[30] Perhaps they have been seen as the province of old salts and rugged seafaring folk—men of the ilk of the old whalers, who often made up their crews. Certainly they do not have the associations of domesticity that endear many early lighthouses to contemporary enthusiasts. But it is also true that there simply are no nineteenth-century light vessels that survive on the waters of the Chesapeake Bay (or, for that matter, elsewhere) to awaken historical curiosity. Yet the employment of manned lightships in United States' waters—which began in 1820 on the Chesapeake Bay—is directly tied to the evolution of engineering and technical capabilities in the construction of lighthouses and other aids to navigation.

Throughout the one hundred sixty-four-year history of their use—from 1820 to 1984—the lightship was often the first beacon to mark dangerous shoals or hazardous coastal approaches.[31] Thus, on the Chesapeake Bay, an aging lighthouse now stands (or, more frequently, formerly stood) at many spots once deemed accessible only to lightships. Their

Continued on page 23

21

CLAY ISLAND 1832-1892

The lighthouse was placed at the tip of Clay Island on a narrow spit of land between the Nanticoke River and Fishing Bay on Maryland's Eastern Shore. The dwelling, with tower on top, was almost the same design as the lighthouse at Greenbury Point near Annapolis. The lighthouse was another of John Donahoo's structures. He was the only bidder (though Pleasanton was always quick to recommend Winslow Lewis if Donahoo did not reduce his price to match the budget). Clay Island was a remote area of the Eastern Shore, yet 6 other lighthouses were eventually constructed within 10 miles of Clay Island. Water traffic was primarily fishing craft out of Crisfield and Deal Island. The point of land at Clay Island is referred to in Daniel Defoe's 18th century novel, *Moll Flanders*. In the book, Moll and her husband (one of many) purchase land on Phillips Point (Clay Island) to establish a plantation. Upon landing at Clay Island, Moll found "no conveniences," but the land was rich. She crossed the Bay numerous times to visit her brother (a one-time husband) who lived up the Rappahannock River.

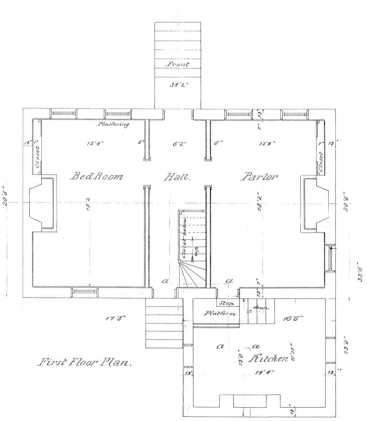

The interior plan of Clay Island placed the 12' x 18' bedroom on the first floor, with a ceiling height of over 8'. The attached kitchen was entered by stepping down from the parlor. The upper floor contained an attic from which a ladder rose, inside the tower, to reach the lantern. Strangely, the 1880 plans called for a 5'10"-high cellar at 4'6" below grade– somewhat questionable specifications for a marshy area well known to have its gravestones occasionally float away at high tide.

In the late 1800s the area around the lighthouse was eroding quickly and the Lighthouse Board pursued plans for a screwpile lighthouse 1 mile south at Sharkfin Shoal to replace Clay Island. The Clay Island light was decommissioned in 1892 and the house left to deteriorate, finally collapsing in 1894.

National Archives Illustrations

extensive use on the Chesapeake Bay, especially during the nineteenth century, may be taken not only as a reminder of the difficulties of navigation, but as a measure of the economic primacy of maritime shipping, especially along north-Atlantic trade routes. For example, well into the first decades of the twentieth century, the Potomac was "so crowded with commercial, passenger, and naval vessels that the opposite shore was hard to see . . ." Regular steamship travel, which began on the Chesapeake in 1813, contributed, in a few short decades, new ships numbering in the hundreds, and greatly increased safety concerns on the Bay.[32]

In the days before construction of open-water lighthouses became feasible, the advantages of the lightship were clear: "[I]t could be moored near shifting shoals where no fixed structure could be placed; stationed in deep water many miles from shore to serve as a landfall or point of departure for transoceanic traffic; and could be readily repositioned to suit changing needs."[33]

The problems of lightships, however, are manifold, beginning with the peculiar engineering difficulties that attend to the construction of ships which, unlike all others, are intended to remain in one spot, and ending with the considerable expense of manning and maintaining vessels that are battered and tossed about by the vagaries of wind and water. They may be torn from their moorings, dragged off station, and even sunk. Thus, as soon as possible lightships were replaced with permanent structures—in the Chesapeake Bay, for example, they were initially superseded by screwpile cottages and caisson towers and, later, by skeletal steel structures and large lighted buoys outfitted with electronic sound, radio and radar equipment.

When compared to England, where a proposal for the placement of lightships was made as early as 1674 (then regarded as "the proposition of a madman"), and where the first lightship was actually introduced to mark the Nore sandbank in the Thames River in 1731,[34] the United States lagged the better part of a century behind, though records from the 1790s mention three floating beacons in

the Chesapeake Bay—on Willoughby Spit, the Horseshoe, and Middle Ground. These probably resembled the "floating beacon with two masts and cages complete" approved for construction by George Washington in 1795—sturdy, turtle-backed, stubby-masted schooners with an iron lantern tended, weather permitting, by someone who rowed out in the evening to light the beacon.[35] The early lights were certainly "very rude and unsatisfactory . . . often blown out, and occasionally blown bodily away."[36] But in 1819 Congress appropriated funds for two lightships proper on the Chesapeake Bay—one to be placed at Willoughby Spit and the other at Wolf Trap Shoal.[37]

The first lightship was ready for service in the summer of 1820 and was placed off Willoughby Spit in the lower Chesapeake near Norfolk where it took such a battering that it was promptly moved to a less exposed position in the Elizabeth River near Craney Island. Even so, the many advantages of the lightship were immediately apparent to all involved in commercial traffic on the Bay. In the same year, additional lightships were authorized for the Chesapeake Bay. By 1821

Certainly the most publicized lightkeeper in Maryland was Fannie Salter of Turkey Point lighthouse, shown here posing for the photographer.

Continued on page 25

23

WATT'S ISLAND 1833-1923

Watt's Island stood offshore from Virginia's Eastern Shore at the meeting of Tangier and Pocomoke Sounds. The lighthouse actually stood on Little Watt's Island just south of the larger Watt's Island. The larger island still exists today, but Little Watt's Island is now a submerged obstruction next to the appropriately named Watt's Island Rocks. The larger island was almost 200 acres when the lighthouse was built in 1833 on the 7 acre Little Watt's Island. One hundred years later the 7 acres had become 3. John Donahoo built the tower and keeper's house. The keeper's house was originally a one-story structure, but in 1891 the Lighthouse Board recommended that "[t]he accommodations for the keepers and their families are insufficient, and it is proposed to build an additional story to the dwelling as has been done at other stations in the district having a similar type of house." The 1893 photo to the left clearly shows the second-story addition and the recently installed fence. It is curious that almost all landbased lighthouses on the Bay used white picket fences. In only 3 years, Board records show that almost 800' feet of fencing was installed at Watt's Island. In 1867, the Board replaced the "old and exceedingly defective" lights at Watt's Island, Clay Island, Fog Point, Turkey Point, Fishing Battery, and Concord Point to "remedy the evil" of inferior lights. The new light installed in Watt's Island's 48' tower was a 5th-order Fresnel lens. Evidence of the Bay's power to move its shores is shown in the top photo where the Bay is at the doorstep of the keeper's house. The light was automated in 1923 and the house abandoned. The final blow came in 1944 when a severe winter storm toppled the tower and demolished the house at Little Watt's Island.

24

lightships were also stationed at Upper Cedar Point, Smith Point, and Wolf Trap.

Little is known about the Bay's early lightships. Certainly, there was scant thought to the specific problems of lightship design—a fact that surely resulted in extraordinary discomfort for their crews. "Early light vessels were largely a product of opinion and arbitrary judgment on the part of builders who were often ignorant of the true purpose of the vessel or its harsh operating environment. For thirty to forty years, therefore, the lightships were exceedingly poor light platforms, their full body, shoal draft, and light displacement combined to cause undue rolling and violent pitching, which resulted in frequent loss of moorings and breakage or damage to the lanterns. By present-day standards, crew accommodations would be judged uninhabitable."[38]

All early lightships were constructed of wood, generally either white oak or live oak. "The tough oak timber . . . was cut from the swamps of southeastern Virginia. Then it was carried to New England where it was sunk in the blue mud of some cove and allowed to season. When her hull was completed it consisted of an outer frame and an inner ceiling. In the space between, salt was poured to harden the wood until it became virtually petrified."[39] Remarkably, in the second decade of the twentieth century, twelve such early lightships were still in service (the last was retired in 1930), and were then thought to be good for another fifty or more years. Sadly, none has survived. Two wooden ships, according to one Coast Guard historian, provided bonfires at Fourth of July celebrations; other early lightships were used as target ships by the Navy; still others were sold.[40]

From the beginning, lightships carried large hand-struck fog bells. During the 1850s, these bells were often supplemented with guns—then thought to provide unusually penetrating sound—but the "obvious hazards of fire, from storing and handling explosive materials, brought a rapid end to these small cannon."[41]

The number of lightships grew continuously during the first half of the nineteenth

century (in 1825 there were ten, more than half of them on the Chesapeake Bay; by 1839 there were thirty, and in 1858 there were forty-eight), and then began to dwindle as inside stations were replaced—as happened on the Chesapeake following the Civil War—by screwpile structures.

Discomfort for the crew was the hallmark of lightship service—as one nineteenth century observer commented, "a term of solitary confinement combined with the horrors of sea-sickness."[42] Often the ships were reoutfitted schooners—extremely difficult to hold on position. So, too, their reflector lights were difficult to maintain in the pitch and roll of waves. Generally, there were eight lamps and a corresponding number of twelve-inch reflectors. These were set upon a ring encircling the mast and enclosed by a glass-paned lantern that could be raised and lowered for servicing. During the day, the lantern was lowered into "a small house, with opening roof, on deck at the base of the mast."[43] At night, the lamps were lighted and the whole apparatus hoisted to the masthead. The best lights were Argand lamps and reflectors supported on their circular frame with gimbals allowing them to swing in response to the ship's motion, but apparently few of the early U.S. lightships were so equipped.[44]

Early lightship construction suffered from the same general inattention to quality that affected the rest of the lighthouse establishment: a lack of investment in design, poor workmanship, and use of inferior construc-

In 1893, the lightship on station at Bush Bluff in the Elizabeth River, Virginia was the converted 80' Coast & Geodetic survey schooner, *Drift*.

Continued on page 27

25

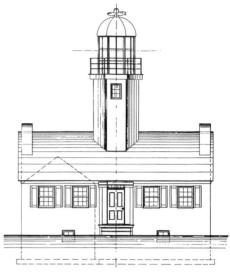

GREENBURY POINT 1849-1934 Greenbury Point is situated at the mouth of the Severn River entering the harbor of Annapolis, Maryland. The point is known today as the location of radio towers just across the point from the U.S. Naval Academy. The first light at Greenbury Point was erected in 1849 after the Lighthouse Board purchased just over two acres of land for $367. No right-of-way to the lighthouse was purchased because Pleasanton preferred that the keeper use his boat. The house was another of the 20'x34' structures supporting a rooftop lantern that were common in the early years of Bay lighthouse construction.

Greenbury Point had two unique design elements: its tower was completely sheathed with wood shingles, and a fish-shaped weathervane was mounted above the lantern. The original light used 9 lamps with parabolic reflectors, but in 1855 this system was replaced by a locomotive lamp, then in use with steam engines. The small railroad lamp proved difficult to see over the lights of the developing Annapolis Harbor and the new Naval Academy buildings. In addition the water frontage was eroding. For years, the Board asked Congress for money to replace the lighthouse. Finally, in1891, a new screwpile lighthouse was placed offshore on the nearby shoal. The cottage-style lighthouse was similar in design to both Hoopers Strait lighthouse (now at the Chesapeake Bay Maritime Museum) and to Drum Point lighthouse (at the Calvert Marine Museum). The hexagonal house was painted white with a brown roof and a black lantern that housed a 4th-order Fresnel lens showing a fixed white light. The light was automated and the house removed in 1934. It stood just about where today's sailboat race starting lines are located. Annapolis is known as America's Sailing Capital and Greenbury Point and the radio towers on the point are familiar to yachtsmen around the world. Most of the WWII towers are scheduled to be demolished, but mariners have requested that at least one of them remain as a guide into Annapolis harbor.

tion materials. Progress lagged far behind the lightships of Northern Europe.[45] An 1838 report to Congress "gave evidence of large scale mismanagement, low morale, incompetence among personnel, and irresponsible performance by contractors." The report also found "that the published range of visibility for all lights was erroneous; that there was no uniform system for coloring, numbering or otherwise identifying floating aids; that the positions of many lightships had been poorly selected; and that additional light vessels were required."[46]

"In 1842, the thirty lightships in service ranged from 40 to 230 tons burden, constructed entirely of wood, poorly rigged in many cases, and seldom with any means at all for propulsion. Illuminating apparatus was limited to multiple-wick sperm oil lamps of poor visibility, and mounted in lanterns, which had to be raised and lowered to the deck for servicing. Ground tackle was inadequate, and hull design still had failed to consider the weather and sea conditions encountered by these small vessels. Neither tender nor relief vessels were available at the time, and as a consequence, when the vessels were frequently blown adrift, stations remained unmarked for periods measured in weeks and months."[47]

Between 1838 and 1842, a number of investigations and reports to Congress led to some improvements in the care and construction of lightships: there was, for example, an attempt to standardize the painting scheme of lightships and buoys, and in each district a revenue cutter—precursor to the lighthouse tender—was made available to the naval officer, who was now assigned to carry out inspections. Still, there was no provision of relief vessels and a lightship towed in for repair would leave its station dangerously dark.

During this period—in fact, until shortly after the Civil War—lightships were identified by their station name or, less frequently, by the name of a prominent citizen—a notable, for example, such as Pleasonton himself. Still, there were no specific directives for identifying lightships. "Although station names were painted on the sides of lightships at about

Coast Guard

Life on lightships veered between excesses—on the one hand, boredom, on the other, dangerous work. Seamen on early lightships were required to go aloft in any kind of weather to work on the lamps raised high on the mast.

this time, neither numbers nor letters were used to identify individual vessels until 1867."[48] Though sometimes erroneously used for identification, the numbers given in light lists were numbers assigned in the publication itself, not numbers given to the lightships. Thus, from 1820 to 1867, the identification, subsequent movement and eventual fate of many U.S. light vessels is largely obscured.

In the beginning, the problems faced by captains, mates and crew members of Chesapeake Bay lightships were somewhat different than those of later lightships or the later years of lightship service on outside positions, for, in spite of the physical discomfort of most lightships on the Bay, there was little of the isolation that characterized lightship duty on outside stations. In fact, most personnel problems related to the absence of crew members from their ships. Land was in sight, and it beckoned.

The hierarchical organization of the lightship crew (of approximately ten—sometimes fewer on inside stations) was roughly the same as any merchant vessel of the day. The basic division was one between the captain's watch and the mate's watch. The daily routine was also fairly simple. At sunrise, the lamp was lowered, and, once the light had been cleaned and readied for the evening's lighting, there was little to do but

27

LIGHTSHIP STATIONS OF THE CHESAPEAKE BAY

STATION NAME	LOCATION	TIME PERIOD	SHIP'S NUMBERS
Craney Island	Eizabeth River	1820-1859	C, Q, R,#21 &23
Upper Cedar Point*	Potomac River narrows	1821-1867	LL,EE,SS & #21
Wolf Trap**	Wolf Trap Shoal	1821-1895	S,T ,& #22
Smith Point*	Entrance, Potomac River	1821-1897	B & #23, 46
Lower Cedar Point*	Potomac River narrows	1825-1867	DD & #24
Hoopers Strait	Entrance, Honga River	1827-1867	#25
Windmill Point*	Entrance Rappahannock	1834-1869	U, ?, Relief
Bowlers Rock**	Rappahannock River	1835 1868	O & #28
Janes Island	Little Annemessex River	1853-1867	Unknown Number
York Spit*	Entrance, York River	1856-1869	#12, T & 21
Choptank River	Choptank River	1870-1872	#25
Cape Charles/Chesapeake	Entrance to Bay	1888-1965	#46,49,101,80,72,116
Bush Bluff	Elizabeth River	1891-1918	#46, *Holly*, #97
Tail of the Horseshoe	Inside Bay entrance	1900-1922	#71 & #46
35 Foot Channel	Mid Bay, off Back River	1908-1919	#45
Cape Charles/Chesapeake	Entrance to Bay	1918-1919	*Owl* & *Brant*, (USN-WWI)

Until 1867, lightships were generally referred to by the name of the station that was often painted on the side of the hull. After 1867 all lightships were given a permanent number, while the station's name could be changed depending on the station served. The number of the vessel shown in the right-hand column refers to the vessel's actual number or, if numbers were not used at the time, to an arbitrary letter designation assigned to the vessel by the Bureau of Lighthouses in 1938. Names in italics refer to vessels temporarily assigned to the station.

* = Lightships that were either captured or removed from their stations by Confederate Forces during the Civil War.
** = Lightships burned or sunk by the Confederate Forces during the Civil War
Note: Not all relief lightships are shown.

© EASTWIND PUBLISHING

---

clean ship or go on watch 'til sundown. Boredom was difficult to overcome. In some ways, too, the "floating lights," as they were then called, were conceptualized as just that—especially when fair weather or spring planting called their crews to other pursuits.

Another source of difficulty in the management of the Bay's lightships was the same practice of political appointment which operated to the detriment of lighthouse stations. Sometimes lightship masters proved their lack of maritime experience under difficult conditions and there were numerous complaints to that effect. Occasionally, a captain was fired. In 1843, for example, the keeper of Lower Cedar Point lightship was dismissed for leaving his vessel "to work in his several farms ashore, leaving four Negroes, in charge who in turn left the vessel allowing pillaging of vessel by vandals and thieves."[49] Likewise, one captain of the Upper Cedar Point lightship was hired and fired many times over a period of nineteen years for failure to tend the light. In 1849, yet another captain was absent with his crew when a schooner rammed the ship.[50] Even so, he was able to stay on as captain until 1853 when the Board began to take a close look at the Chesapeake Bay's lightship personnel.

Absenteeism was not a problem on all early Bay lightships, and it is important to note that the weather — as well as the unsuitability of many ships— gave many a captain and crew ample opportunity to test their mettle and mariner's skills. More than one lightship was carried off station by floes of ice; the ribs of other ships were likewise crushed.[51]

During the 1851 investigation of the lighthouse establishment, Pleasonton was particularly vague and defensive in his replies regarding the then-numerous "floating lights,"—so much so that in a letter to Secretary of Treasury Thomas Corwin dated June 16, 1851, Commodore William Bradford Shubrick, head of the fledgling Lighthouse Board, complained: "[T]he information provided in the reply of the Fifth Auditor . . . is not an answer to the queries . . .."[52]

Pleasonton's second reply provided little more in the way of precise information. ". . . [W]e have," he noted, "forty-one [floating lights] stations in the Delaware and Chesapeake Bays, the sounds of North Carolina, and at different places at sea . . .."[53] "The mode of lighting them has advantages over that adopted in the British service," Pleasonton avowed, but the Board scoffed at the presumption of any technological superiority. "The floating lights of the United States are all fixed, and fitted with common torch lamps . . . far inferior to those of England and Ireland in brilliancy, range, useful effect, and certainty of being found at all times in their proper position."[54]

The expense of maintaining light vessels was very likely a matter of particular irritation to Pleasonton, but the Board was more impressed by the expense occasioned by lack of upkeep and poor supervision. "The want of care and attention in wetting the decks and keeping them clean, scrubbing the vessels outside, and keeping them properly painted and well ventilated, will account for the rapid decay of them . . .."[55] The boats were not properly moored and many traveled in large circles around their anchors, "destroying...[their] usefulness as a range."[56] In sum, they stated flatly, "Nothing could be much worse than the floating lights of the United States."[57]

The recommendations of the Lighthouse Board were precise: that all light-vessels "be fitted with the best system of lamps and para-

bolic reflectors; both for fixed and revolving lights;" that "attention be given to the subject of models for light-vessels, constructing and mooring them, so as to give greater assurance to the navigator that they will always be found in position;" that light-vessels "be painted and fitted with distinguishing marks by day, to enable the mariner to know them without difficulty;" and, finally, that "relief vessels be placed on stations whenever a light-vessel is removed for repair"; and, "in the event of a light-vessel parting her moorings, then that position be occupied without delay by a substitute."[58]

But in one respect, at least, Pleasonton correctly stated the opinion of all subsequent agencies that have had occasion to take charge of the country's aids to navigation—from the Lighthouse Board and the Bureau of Lighthouses, to the Coast Guard: "Light vessels," he noted, "ought never to be adopted for any situation in which a lighthouse can be built for any reasonable sum, for they are not only driven from their moorings often when they are most wanted, but in the frequent and expensive repairs that they require, and in the large number of men necessarily kept on board of them, they are three or four times the annual expense of a light-house of the first class."[59]

Congress lost no time in formalizing the administrative apparatus of the Lighthouse Board. Historians do not note what became of Stephen Pleasonton, though it is fairly certain that the rationale for much of his administration had been lost—even to him—when Winslow Lewis died in 1850 at the age of eighty. If Pleasonton had possessed even a small fraction of Lewis's inventiveness and progressive entrepreneurial energy, the U.S. lighthouse establishment might not have languished in the 1830s and 1840s. "It is time," the Investigating Committee of the Board told Congress in 1852, "that this subject received full and careful investigation by experiment under the direction of scientific men."[60] They were about to have their say.

Pleasonton correctly noted:"Lightvessels ought never be adopted for any situation in which a lighthouse can be built for any reasonable sum."

29

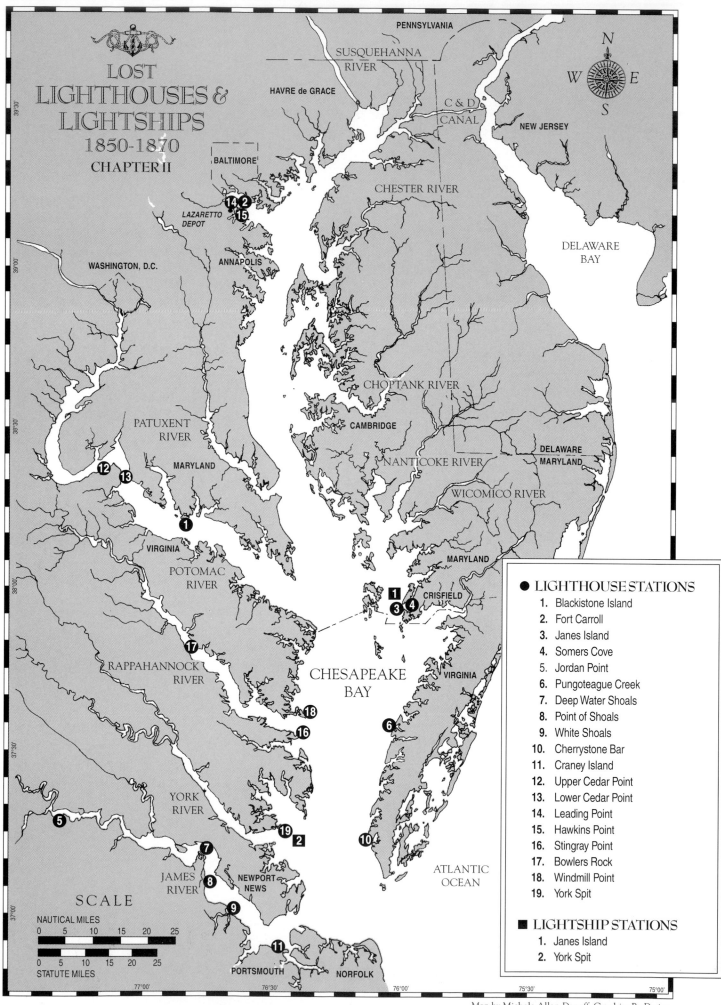

LOST LIGHTHOUSES & LIGHTSHIPS
1850-1870
CHAPTER II

PENNSYLVANIA

SUSQUEHANNA RIVER

HAVRE de GRACE

C & D CANAL

NEW JERSEY

BALTIMORE

LAZARETTO DEPOT

CHESTER RIVER

DELAWARE BAY

WASHINGTON, D.C.

ANNAPOLIS

CHOPTANK RIVER

PATUXENT RIVER

CAMBRIDGE

MARYLAND

NANTICOKE RIVER

DELAWARE
MARYLAND

VIRGINIA

WICOMICO RIVER

POTOMAC RIVER

MARYLAND

CRISFIELD

RAPPAHANNOCK RIVER

CHESAPEAKE BAY

VIRGINIA

YORK RIVER

NEWPORT NEWS

ATLANTIC OCEAN

JAMES RIVER

SCALE

NAUTICAL MILES
0 5 10 15 20 25

STATUTE MILES
0 5 10 15 20 25

PORTSMOUTH   NORFOLK

● LIGHTHOUSE STATIONS
1. Blackistone Island
2. Fort Carroll
3. Janes Island
4. Somers Cove
5. Jordan Point
6. Pungoteague Creek
7. Deep Water Shoals
8. Point of Shoals
9. White Shoals
10. Cherrystone Bar
11. Craney Island
12. Upper Cedar Point
13. Lower Cedar Point
14. Leading Point
15. Hawkins Point
16. Stingray Point
17. Bowlers Rock
18. Windmill Point
19. York Spit

■ LIGHTSHIP STATIONS
1. Janes Island
2. York Spit

Map by Michele Allan Danoff, Graphics By Design.

CHAPTER II

When the Lighthouse Board was formally constituted as a branch of the Treasury Department in 1852, the new nine-member board set to work with a practical zeal that characterized its entire fifty-eight year history—though their zealousness, some would say, became less practical and more self-congratulatory in the waning days of the nineteenth century.

From a small organization of fifty-five lighthouses in 1820, the lighthouse establishment turned over to the nine-member Lighthouse Board had increased to three hundred thirty-one lighthouses and forty-two lightships. Of this number, twenty-four lighthouses (all but the North Point range land-based) and eight lightships (all of them on inside stations) were active navigational aids on the Chesapeake Bay.

Based on its 1851 investigation, the Lighthouse Board had a clear idea not only of the design of the equipment they wanted to install and the quality of the light that they wanted to show, but also of the responsibilities and routine of keepers, and this in round-the-clock detail.[1] In all matters, supervision (which had heretofore been almost entirely absent) was to be close and strict. Twelve new lighthouse districts were created and a naval officer was appointed as inspector to each. Within a few years, a district engineer had also been added to oversee repair and new construction. Now the light stations were inspected every three months.

In matters of personnel management, the Lighthouse Board ran an exceedingly tight ship, and in this, as most lighthouse historians have observed, there was a strong military influence originating in the makeup of the Board itself. Even so, the nature of the Board's personnel administration did change through time. Initially, the Board concerned itself more with the improvement of the light and with the care and use of the equipment, supplies, and tools that it provided. Included in their detailed inventories and directives to keepers were precise instructions for use of such things as "the dusting and feather brushes, linen aprons, rouge powder, prepared whiting, spirits of wine, buff or chamois skins, and linen cleaning cloths."[2] The days when a lighthouse keeper might be found with no means to measure oil, tell time, and no trimming scissors were over—or, put another way, the days when the lightkeeper came to the job with his own tools and ideas about how to use them had come to an end. In fact, precious little was left to the keeper's judgment, for the Lighthouse Board quickly established a measurement, instruction and timeframe regarding every item and activity of the daily routine, a trend that continued over the next twenty years, so that the position of lighthouse keeper was qualitatively changed from one of almost complete independence from supervision to one of detailed regulation of every activity connected with the light. Seen in historical perspective, these changes are of great interest because they predate similar changes in the organization of wage labor in industrial production by almost fifty years.

Another closely related problem requiring the immediate attention of the Lighthouse Board concerned purchasing: standardization of supplies, quality control, and delivery of material needed at the growing number of lighthouse stations. On Staten Island, New York, a central supply depot was quickly set up for the entire lighthouse service and was soon followed by the establishment of depots

During this period, the Chesapeake Bay lighthouse establishment grew into one of the largest and, overall, probably the most complex aids to navigation system in the United States.

31

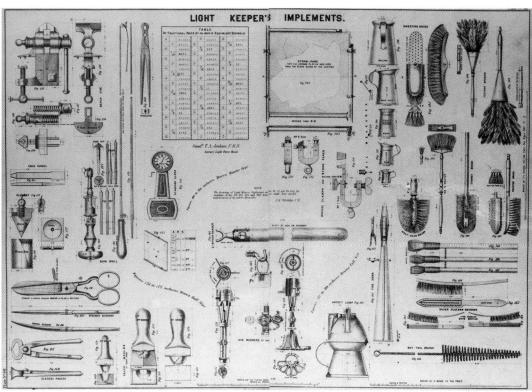

LIGHT KEEPER'S IMPLEMENTS.

Implements mandated for use by light keepers ranged from specialized brushes to a fancy "banjo" wall clock.

in each lighthouse district. The first depot on the Chesapeake was at Lazaretto Point, but others followed—Norfolk, Point Lookout, Washington and Annapolis. Nevertheless, Staten Island was retained as the central supply depot (called "the general depot"), purchasing and receiving all manner of goods for transshipment to district depots.[3] Through the centralization of purchasing, greater economy and uniformity in quality were possible. Standards could be set for suppliers, and adherence to these standards could be carefully monitored. In the Chesapeake Bay, supplies from the Staten Island depot were usually delivered by lighthouse tender; supplies to other parts of the country, however, were increasingly conveyed by rail. Either way, the days when one lighthouse tender handled supplies and repairs—on a once-a-year basis—to all U.S. light stations were definitely over.

The screwpile lighthouse began its evolution in eighteenth-century England with lighthouses supported by strong wooden piles. In 1830, a design of cast-iron piles with spiral flanges, which would anchor the lighthouse infrastructure in a sandy or muddy substratum, was patented by Alexander Mitchell, a British engineer. By 1841, screwpile structures had appeared in the Thames and Wyre rivers, and, by 1842, the effectiveness of the design and its ready application to such waters as the Chesapeake and Delaware Bays had been noted by one of the congressionally appointed teams investigating the superiority of European lighthouse establishments. The screwpile's greatest utility for the Chesapeake Bay was that it could be located farther out on the Bay's hazardous shoals—shoals that often extended far beyond the points of land where lighthouse towers could be located. By the 1850s, encroachment of the Bay had already occasioned the loss of several lighthouse towers and it was recognized that others soon would be lost or would require extensive bulwarking to protect. In addition, the Bay's towers had too often been at considerable distance from the channels, which ships of deep draft needed to follow if they were to avoid grounding. An inexpensive solution was now deemed at hand.

For the Chesapeake Bay, the adoption of

the screwpile lighthouse was an innovation that quickly altered the face of the Bay. Beginning in the 1850s the Lighthouse Board adopted a policy of replacing the Bay's aging lightships and lighthouses with screwpile structures. After a first disastrous attempt with the Pungoteague River lighthouse, built in 1854 and shorn from its moorings by a field of moving ice in 1856 (actually, only 429 days after it was commissioned), ice breakers and riprap stone were used to prevent ice from piling up around the foundations. Although some lighthouses still met a similar fate in the frozen waters of the Bay, it is a mistake to think that the structures were fragile; in fact, most survived the vagaries of Chesapeake weather and succumbed only when the push for unmanned lighthouse stations made their strong foundations attractive for another kind of light. The design of six to eight flanged cast-iron piles set around a central pile, all tightly screwed into the Bay's substratum and braced with rolled iron bars which, in turn, supported another level of structural cast-iron posts and beams, proved remarkably worthy.

On the Chesapeake Bay, the timber-framed cottages with dormer windows and a roof-top lantern were generally of square or hexagonal design and were surrounded by a large porch deck with wooden handrails and balusters and a lantern deck or catwalk with matching balustrade. Though charming in appearance, the cottages offered precious little living space for the keeper and his family. Generally, the stations and the families that lived in them were closely tied to communities on shore, especially along the western rivers of the Chesapeake, for example, Upper and Lower Cedar Point on the Potomac and Jordan Point, White Shoals, Point of Shoals, and Deep Shoals on the James.

If one looks at the bibliography of the Lighthouse Board's 1852 tome, one notices that the overwhelming number of references are to European books and reports, the greatest number of them French. In fact, the French system was the model most emulated by the Board, beginning with adoption of "the Board" itself—an administrative entity that was

Continued on page 37

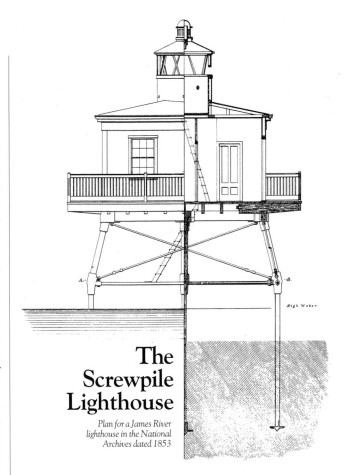

The Screwpile Lighthouse

Plan for a James River lighthouse in the National Archives dated 1853

The Bay's shallow protected waters and soft bottom were ideal for planting the spidery legs of screwpile structures. The depth of the pilings varied with the solidity of the substratum, but were usually driven no more than 6'. The tapered iron pilings were 6"-10" in diameter and the corkscrew like blades at their ends were 2'-3' from tip to tip with a 10" or 12" pitch. The blades guided and twisted the pilings into the bottom and were capable of penetrating most substrate, except very hard surfaces.

The number of legs varied according to the house, depth of water, strength of the current, and bottom configuration of the site. The network of framing underneath lighthouses often looks as though it is a screwpile, when in fact some Bay lighthouses, such as Pages Rock and Deep Water Shoal, had pilings made of wood inside cast-iron sleeves. These were driven deeply into the bottom of the Bay, and often stabilized with large metal disks at the surface.

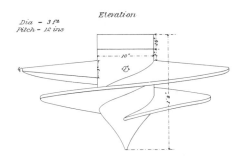

33

c. 1931, Coast Guard

BLACKISTONE ISLAND 1851-1956 *St. Clement's or Blakistone Island* One of the last lighthouses built by John Donahoo, the original brick lighthouse was commissioned in November, 1851. In its first 8 years of operation, the light station had 3 keepers. In 1859, Jerome McWilliams, son of the island's owner, Joseph L. McWilliams, was appointed keeper and remained until 1875. Though official keeper, McWilliams apparently encouraged other family members to take care of his lighthouse duties. McWilliams was followed by his sister, Josephine Freeman, whose tenure as lightkeeper lasted until 1911.

Perhaps no other story better illustrates the cross-cutting ties that bound the North and South in the tidewater region than the story of its raid in 1864 by Captain John Goldsmith—who was himself a former owner of the island—and his rebel party of twelve. According to local St. Mary's County historian, David Norris, after destroying the lens and lamp and absconding with the oil, the raiding party apparently intended to dynamite the building. Some say that McWilliams pleaded successfully on behalf of his pregnant wife; others suggest that Goldsmith and McWilliam knew each other.

At any rate, after the skirmish, it was not the stalwart keeper but rather the pregnant, near-term Mrs. McWilliams and her sister-in-law who tended the light until Federal forces arrived from nearby Point Lookout. Soldiers remained at the site and a Federal gunboat cruised nearby until the war ended. Following the Civil War, the island was developed by the McWilliams family: a steamship pier was built, the house was expanded to take in boarders, and, finally, a bath house and cottages were built. Apparently, it was now the elder McWilliams who was taking care of lighthouse duties while other family members grew seasonal crops and fished and farmed the

c. 1931, Coast Guard

waters for oysters, all of which the steamships carried to nearby markets. Business boomed, a hotel was built, and the elder McWilliams became more ambitious still, laying out a veritable town of subdivided lots and named streets which he offered for sale through a Washington lawyer.

But the island's boom period was not to last. An 1889 freshet virtually destroyed the oyster beds and, shortly thereafter, McWilliams's ventures began to founder and the island, which was rapidly losing land area, was mortgaged and began to change hands. Under new ownership, some reconstruction of the old prosperity was attempted: 3 new cottages were built, a small tomato canning factory was put into operation. In 1919 the island was taken over by the Navy. The owner was kept on as caretaker and allowed to pursue his family's livelihood--though changes on the island made this difficult. The fruit orchards were razed, the pond was filled, and a landing field was constructed. By now, there were only 66 acres remaining (the island was originally surveyed at 400).

The lighthouse was fully automated in 1932, a time when automation was overtaking many Chesapeake lights. Thereafter, the structure began to deteriorate until, on July 16, 1956, a fire gutted the building and raged across the island. A local newspaper article suggested that ordnance from the nearby Naval Proving Ground started the fire. Some residents reported seeing a shell burst near the island. And residents also reported seeing smoke coming from the island as early as 8 a.m., but the fire department was not called until 6 o'clock in the evening. By the time firefighters could be ferried to the island with portable equipment, the lighthouse was beyond repair, and, deeming the structure a danger, the Navy, which may or may not have been responsible for the fire, finished the job with dynamite, scattering the lighthouse bricks and twisted pieces of the catwalk railing over a wide arc along the island's shores. *Sources: Frederick Tilp, 1974; David Norris, 1994.*

A 1851 survey of Blackistone Island (now called St. Clement's Island) shows the light station on just over 2 acres on the southern tip of the 22 acre island. The 1935 photo above shows the nearby cross built in 1934 to recognize the site of Leonard Calvert's 1634 landing on the island, now considered the birthplace of Maryland. *Calvert Marine Museum photo*

35

FORT CARROLL 1854-1931 The Fort Carroll light station, built in 1854, identified the channel to the south side of the heavy granite bulwarks of the 6-sided, 4-acre fort. Offshore, and to the west of Sparrows Point, the light marked a turning point in the channel leading into Baltimore Harbor. Preparations for the construction of the fort (intended to follow Fort McHenry as Baltimore's second line of defense) began in 1847 with the lessons of the War of 1812 in mind—lessons which turned out to be obsolete. In 1848, Robert E. Lee, then a brevet-colonel in the Army Corps of Engineers and just returned from the Mexican War, was sent to supervise the construction. For 3 years before his appointment as superintendent of West Point, he commuted daily to the fort from Baltimore. Plans called for a 4-story structure of tiered galleries which could hold 350 cannon, but Congress had second thoughts about the construction of such an elaborate fort so far north of the Virginia Capes and, after the completion of the 1st tier, appropriations were placed on hold.

In 1854, the light in a small 6th-order Fresnel lens was lit in the frame tower. At this time, the keeper and his family were the only residents on the fort. As with Fort Washington on the Potomac, the lightkeepers were subservient to the military command—a matter of little consequence at Fort Carroll until the outbreak of the Spanish-American War. Occasional repairs are noted in the annual reports—painting, new glass for the lantern, the purchase of a Franklin lamp and a new cooking stove for the keeper, a new water tank and repair to the lightning rod. Of greatest note, was the construction of a new frame tower for the lens and fog-bell machine in 1875, and, in 1888, the completion of a new keeper's dwelling at a cost just over $1,000. "It is a comfortable building," the Board reported, "about 20 by 25 feet in plan, two stories in height, with a porch, and is built of yellow pine." In 1898, a second tower (shown here) was built.

1888 drawing of the keeper's house; the roofline of which is visible in the photo below, to the left of the light tower. The keeper and his family sometimes found themselves in the center of an unusual military presence—surrounded by cannons and soldiers.

The light station was discontinued in 1931 and the island fort sold to a private party. Remnants of the light tower remain today.

1960, Maryland Historical Society

In the 1950s Fort Carroll was sold to a Baltimore attorney who planned to open the fort and lighthouse as a tourist attraction. It never happened and the lantern tower and fort are about to fall in the Patapsco River.

to combine "all the scientific experience necessary to the highest success in illumination, construction hydrography, engineering, knowledge of the needs of commerce, and especially of administration."[4] Not surprisingly, the beautiful and expensive Fresnel lens was meant to be the visible centerpiece of the new service, and the Lighthouse Board "pushed its substitution with vigor."[5]

The superiority of Augustin Fresnel's lens consisted "in surrounding the lamp by a series of prismatic rings of glass, each different from the others in its angles, but all cut mathematically to such angles that the rays that go above the proper plane and those that fall below [are] bent by refraction and reflection so as to become parallel with the lateral rays. Thus, all the rays are saved and sent out in one sheet over the ocean."[6] Actually, the prismatic lenses often covered an arc of less than 360 degrees, especially those manufactured for shore-based towers, and on the darkened side a mirror that reflected the light back into the refracting prisms would be placed. The Board made much of the fact that the light "could be managed by the average light-keeper after instruction by an expert,"[7] but of greatest importance was the anticipation that the new lenticular apparatus would produce a marked savings in oil, requiring only about one-quarter the amount used with the old

lamps and reflectors. Thus, it could easily claim that the new lens would pay for itself in a matter of a few years. The illuminants also underwent several changes, beginning in 1851 with the switch from whale sperm oil to colza oil (rape-seed), and then, because efforts to interest farmers in growing rape seed had largely failed, to lard oil. (Because of its extreme flammability, kerosene was long considered a dangerous substitute to the traditional animal and vegetable oils and was only gradually introduced, after a long period of experimentation that began in the 1870s.)

Of the six possible orders of lights (the sixth being the smallest), most lighthouse stations on the Chesapeake Bay—with the exception of the Cape Charles and Cape Henry lights at the mouth of the Bay—showed a fourth or fifth-order light. The fourth-order lens was eighteen inches in diameter and cost between $350 and $1230, depending on the arc of visibility required. The fifth-order light was only fourteen inches in diameter and priced between $230 and $840. In contrast, the magnificent first-order lenses installed at the Cape Charles and Cape Henry towers had a diameter of six feet and a height of ten feet and cost somewhere between $4,250 and $8,400.[8] The lamps were likewise graded, the fourth-order lamp with a single one-and-a-half inch circular wick and burning one-and-a-half

Continued on page 39

37

JANES ISLAND 1853-1867-1935

James Island, Maryland station (the island has been called Janes or James, changing its name almost with the tide for no apparent reason) began with a lightship in 1853 protecting the bar running out from Island Point off what is now Janes Island State Park. Within sight was the fishing community of Crisfield, then known as the seafood capital of America. The lightship was 76' long, painted cream with black letters. She was apparently not very well built, for she had to be retired due to severe leaking and was replaced with a relief ship in 1866. It was suggested by many that a lighthouse be placed on the bar to begin with, but Pleasonton succumbed to local pressure for a lightship. After one year's service by the relief ship, a screwpile lighthouse was placed on station, but only 12 years later it was destroyed by ice flow. The second lighthouse (opposite) was also destroyed by ice in 1935 and local folk remember seeing the superstructure floating for days in Tangier Sound before it finally sank. It was replaced by the simple, sturdy automatic light and bell built on a cylindrical caisson, shown below.

If you ask around Crisfield about the Jane's Island lightship, Maryland watermen like to tell the following tale:

It seems a Virginia waterman was coming into Crisfield when he spotted the newly anchored lightship. Assuming the big ship had run aground on the bar, the waterman asked the captain if he needed a tow. The captain responded that he was a lightship and a tow was not needed, upon which the waterman yelled back; "I don't give a damn if you're light or heavy, I can tow ya."

Coast Guard

Mariners' Museum   *Sterling Evans, Smith Island*

Coast Guard

SOMERS COVE 1867-1932

The lighthouse at Somers Cove was placed on station to lead mariners into Crisfield harbor, shown in the background of this 1915 photo. It was a small square cottage-style structure with vertical lap siding—the least expensive class of lighthouse, costing less than $10,000. The house itself was only 20'7" x 21', and its tower contained a small 6th-order lamp. The lighthouse was demolished in 1932.

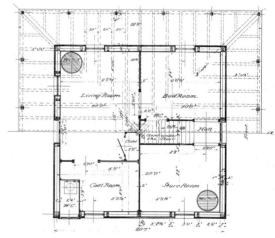

National Archives

gills of oil per hour (214 gallons annually), and the first-order lamp containing five concentric wicks between one and four-and-a-half inches and consuming fifteen gills of oil hourly (or 2,156 gallons annually).[9]

The purchase of new lamps and Fresnel lenses freed up the best parabolic reflectors and Argand lamps for use on lightships—and this was perhaps the first material improvement made on the ships that dotted the Bay and Atlantic coastal waters. But the institutionalized review of all plans, contracts and material purchases also meant that the ships that the Board purchased or had built were of far better quality. Finally, the close supervision of the district engineer—and, in turn, his close supervision by the Board—meant that contract specifications in the construction of lightships (as well as lighthouses) were likely to be carried out to the letter.

Theoretically, at least, the Board was interested in improving the design of lightships and began to wrestle with the peculiar engineering problems that these ships presented. Clearly, they also recognized the advisability of having lightships with some motive power (like the tenders that they purchased and built to serve them), not only to get the lightvessels on station (or back on station if blown off), but to help keep them on station in rough weather. In 1852, the "Committee on Light-Vessels, Etc." was specifically charged with "all subjects relating to light-vessels . . . including plans, models, estimates, contracts, materials, modes of construction, improvement, moorings, fog-signals, and other accessories, and the keepers, seamen, and others employed."[10] Though they began their researches right away, and though new designs were tried and employed in lightship construction, it was some thirty years before other changes were finally put into effect. Likewise, the committee on lightships debated the merits of iron-cladding for ships kept on station year round, but throughout this period, the lightships continued to be built of oak—thought to be stronger and more resilient under protracted stress. Wood was also thought to "breathe," an important consideration at a time when

Before any screwpile lighthouse could be built, soundings of the density of the bottom would be taken by engineers.

National Archives

good ventilation was believed the most important preventative of on-board sickness—and a time when there was great fear of infectious disease in sea-faring towns and cities.

Two new lightship stations, Janes Island (1853-1867) and York Spit (1855-1870), were established (and discontinued) during this period. In truth, the Chesapeake lightships were largely doomed before the outbreak of the Civil War because the Board saw in the screwpile lighthouse a more stable light and, certainly, a much more economical means of lighting the Bay and its tributaries. Judging from the number of new screwpile lighthouses built in the 1850s, it is difficult to know whether the removal and sinking of Chesapeake Bay lightships during the Civil War (two were stripped and burned) hastened or delayed the replacement of inside lightship stations with screwpile structures. Certainly, the determination to replace them had already been made.

The need for more reliable lights was accentuated by the increasing concentration of passenger traffic that ever larger and faster steamships afforded. Gruesome steamboat explosions and collisions, which by the 1850s had occurred up and down the Bay and its

39

National Archives

JORDAN POINT 1855-1927 The original lighthouse at Jordan Point in the upper James River was 1 of 5 lighthouses built in Virginia in 1855. The first lighthouse was a tower-on-house structure which was overcome by shore erosion and demolished in 1875. In the same year, a new fog-bell tower was built and the station's lantern was placed on the top of the new bell tower. A new keeper's dwelling was built in 1888. But the station was still too close to shore and the strong current at the curve of the James River caused continued erosion of the frontage. In 1893, a 412' wall of shore protection was erected, but erosion eventually won out and the house was sold in 1927 for $1,105. Sometime in the 1930s, the house was abandoned and, in 1941, a skeleton tower was placed on the point.

National Archives

The 1875 lamp and fog-bell tower at Jordan Point was a well-proportioned, clapboard structure with more detailed woodwork than the keeper's dwelling.

Coast Guard

rivers, from the Patapsco to the James, had cost many lives, and the safety of passenger traffic was much on the minds of shipowners, captains, maritime engineers, the public and, of course, the members of the Lighthouse Board (much as airline safety is a matter of ongoing concern today). Safety concerns also dictated the acquisition of relief vessels for lightships damaged by collision and storms, or otherwise in need of repair. In the Chesapeake Bay, on at least one occasion, the relief vessel was a temporarily reoutfitted sidewheeler, the *Holly*, ordinarily in service as a tender. (The *Holly*, in fact, enjoyed the greatest longevity of any tender on the Bay.)

Historians differ in their analyses of the tensions that characterized the Chesapeake region in the years immediately preceding the outbreak of war, some of them emphasizing the economic and cultural differences between broad geographical regions—Tidewater, Piedmont and Appalachia—that traversed, north to south, the Potomac River boundary, and others stressing Maryland's growing identification with the North, its financial ties to northern industry, visible, most especially, in Baltimore's investment in railroads and, concomitantly, in transmontane coal and the burgeoning Ohio River Valley. "Between the two states that bordered the Potomac, the river came more and more to be a dividing rather than a uniting force, to acquire the characteristics of a frontier. The Civil War itself, dividing the two states along the frontier of the Potomac, was to mark the tragic climax of that growing disunity."[11]

However briefly, it is important to draw attention to the profound political ambivalence that characterized so much of the Chesapeake region during the Civil War, first of all, because the Lighthouse Board was not immune to these deep stirrings, experiencing confounding stresses, and at all levels of operation. Many Navy officers, including some of the brightest and best, left Washington to offer their services to the Confederacy (for example, "the brilliant and daring" commander Rafael Semmes, who resigned his Navy commission along with his Lighthouse

c.1908, Coast Guard

PUNGOTEAGUE CREEK 1854-1856 The original screwpile lighthouse at Pungoteague Creek, Virginia, was the first screwpile lighthouse built on the Chesapeake Bay and the shortest-lived lighthouse on the Bay. Built in November 1854, the hexagonal structure was overturned by a large mass of floating ice in February 1856. The Lighthouse Board felt that traffic in the area did not justify another lighthouse and, in 1908, the Board built the odd-looking light structure above with the concrete-filled steel caisson on top of the stone rubble of the original screwpile foundation.

Board appointment in February 1861).[12] Throughout the war years, Lighthouse Board reports are terse and detached, unusually devoid of detail regarding keepers, property or events (suggesting almost an unofficial neutrality). In fact, significantly less can be learned about the destruction of lighthouse property on the Chesapeake Bay during the Civil War than that occasioned by bad storms and normal wear and tear in other years.

Second, but of no less importance, broad changes in the perception of the whole Chesapeake region (which, it is to be remembered, only a few decades earlier had seemed to encompass the political heart, economic center and, even, the Western frontier of the young nation), are sometimes subtly (sometimes not so subtly) revealed. By the 1860s, the interests of the railroad magnates and bankers of Baltimore, or, in Washington, of the federal government itself, including the Lighthouse Board, extended across a nation that reached far beyond the state boundaries of either Maryland or Virginia. For capitalist and government bureaucrat alike, the theater of war accelerated the expansion of their activities

Continued on page 45

c.1965 Coast Guard

DEEP WATER SHOALS 1855-1936 Deep Water Shoals, Point of Shoals, White Shoals and Jordan Point lighthouses were all built in 1855 to mark the meandering shoals and bends in Virginia's James River. The 3 screwpile lighthouses built that year were of similar design, and all were raided by the Confederates in the early years of the Civil War. The first screwpile structure at Deep Water Shoals was destroyed by ice in 1867 and a new lighthouse (above) was built on a new frame a year later. Technically not screwpiles, the new frame substituted wooden piles covered with cast-iron sleeves in place of the previously used solid wrought-iron pilings—a technique that would be used on other cottage-style lighthouses on the Bay. The lighthouse was decommissioned in 1936, and dismantled in 1966, during the Coast Guard's automation program.

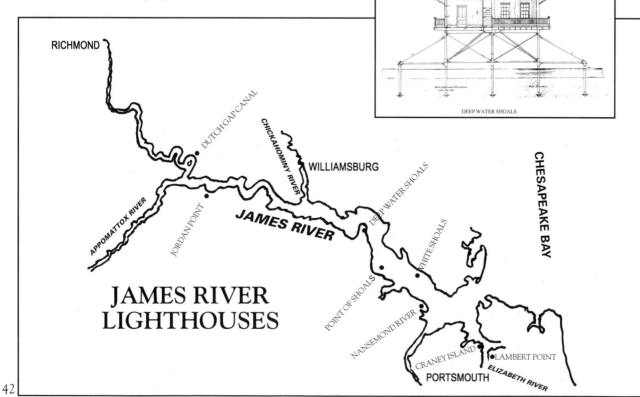

DEEP WATER SHOALS

RICHMOND

DUTCH GAP CANAL

CHICKAHOMINY RIVER

WILLIAMSBURG

APPOMATTOX RIVER

JORDAN POINT

JAMES RIVER

DEEP WATER SHOALS

WHITE SHOALS

CHESAPEAKE BAY

JAMES RIVER LIGHTHOUSES

POINT OF SHOALS

NANSEMOND RIVER

CRANEY ISLAND

LAMBERT POINT

PORTSMOUTH

ELIZABETH RIVER

Mariners' Museum

POINT OF SHOALS 1855-1933 Point of Shoals was built on the firm bottom of Burwell's Bay on the shallow southern shoreline of the James River. It was a hexagonal screwpile cottage of the same basic design as White Shoals and Deep Water Shoals lights. Ice damaged the first screwpile structure and it was rebuilt in 1871. The shoaling under the light became severe as the channel was moved more to the center of the river. The lighthouse became unnecessary and was demolished in the early 1930s.

WHITE SHOALS 1855-1934 White Shoals light was in the middle of the James River just above Newport News. The Lighthouse Inspector of the 5th District reported in 1869: "This is a screwpile of the oldest and most inferior design. It is proposed to rebuild [it] after the design of the lighthouse lately erected on Deep Water Shoal." It appears that the iron-sleeved wooden pilings of Deep Water Shoals lighthouse became the Board's hope for the problem of ice flow in the James River. White Shoals was rebuilt in 1871 and it remained in service until the 1930s, when it was replaced by a steel tower placed nearby.

Many of the James River lights were removed by the Union and stored at Fort Monroe after the Union Army of the Potomac withdrew from the area in 1862. The light fixtures at Deep Water Shoals, Point of Shoals and White Shoals were actually large pressed-glass masthead lights that the Board had found adequate for river navigation.

c. 1885, Coast Guard

CHERRYSTONE BAR 1859-1919 Cherrystone is the only Chesapeake lighthouse to have served at 2 different stations —and, in both Maryland and Virginia. It was originally built to serve the Cherrystone inlet into the town of Cape Charles on Virginia's Eastern Shore. In 1853, according to the Lighthouse Board, Cherrystone was the best harbor in the southeastern part of the Chesapeake Bay. The lighthouse was discontinued in 1919 when the automatic acetylene lantern on a caisson (shown above) was placed nearby. Yet the screwpile lighthouse structure was apparently in good condition, and, in 1920, it was removed from its frame foundation and barged into Cape Charles where it was stored on land for the winter. In the spring of 1921, it was again put on a barge and towed up the Bay to serve for the next 43 years as the light at Benoni Point on Maryland's Choptank River near Cambridge.

Quickly built, and commissioned in 1884, the lighthouse at Craney Island marked one of the oldest stations on the Bay.

CRANEY ISLAND 1820-1859-1936 The station at Craney Island, was just south of the entrance to the Elizabeth River, between Norfolk and Portsmouth, Virginia. Established in 1820 by the first lightship in the United States, the lightship was originally stationed at the northern end of Willoughby Spit, but, unable to endure the strong sea conditions at that location, it was quickly moved to Craney Island. The 70-ton ship was built by James Poole of Hampton, Virginia in 1819. She had 1 fixed light, was lead colored with her name painted on both sides of the hull in large black letters. In 1859 the ship was replaced by a square screwpile lighthouse. The lighthouse was damaged in 1861 by Confederate raiders at about the same time as the U.S. Navy abandoned the nearby Norfolk Navy Yard. A temporary light was shown from the ruins of the lighthouse in 1862. In 1883, the structure was found to be decayed and work began at the Lazaretto Depot to frame a superstructure for a new lighthouse. In short order, a new hexagonal cottage (above) was placed on the old foundation. It lasted until the mid-1930s when it was replaced by a simple light on top of the screwpile foundation.

and broadened their perceptions. For the people of the Chesapeake Bay, the policies that resulted were experienced as the deepest betrayal. "The Civil War scarred Maryland as no other war ever has," one historian has written. "The state was occupied by the North and invaded by the South."[13] In an April 1861 legislative report, drafted in response to a secessionist motion, Maryland's lawmakers "stigmatized Lincoln's calling out of the troops as 'a deliberate summons to the people of two sections into which his party and its principles had so hopelessly divided the land, to shed each other's blood in wantonness and hate.'"[14] With the secession of its western counties and the loss of part of its territory, Virginia tasted equally the bitterness of division.

It is illustrative to briefly consider some of the events of early 1861 in Baltimore, the Bay's most northern metropolis, whose rapidly expanding industrial interests are often cited as pivotal in keeping Maryland in the Union. Though from the perspective of investment capital, Baltimore City was strongly allied with the North (and perhaps with the lucrative prospect of war itself), the civilian population was stirred by intense ambivalence. The preceding summer, two nominating conventions were held in Baltimore (the two becoming three because of yet another splinter). But when the election votes were tallied, Lincoln—nominated at the Republican convention in Chicago—came in a distant fourth with only 2,295 Maryland votes. By early January of 1861, detachments of Marines had been stationed at Fort Washington (the Virginia side of the Potomac) and at Baltimore's Fort McHenry. Thereafter, the occupation of strategic Maryland positions by Union forces—the consolidation of the federal stronghold—continued aggressively.

On April 19, two days after the Virginia secession, street riots broke out in Baltimore

45

Continued on page 49

c. 1890, Maryland Historical Society

LAZARETTO LIGHTHOUSE DEPOT 1863-1958

Though a lighthouse had been in operation since 1831 at Lazaretto Point, it was not made a depot station until 1863. It was not a grand opening, what with the Union Army storing ordnance on most of the property. After the Civil War, the Board began looking at other depot sites, aware that Lazaretto's lack of space would restrict its usefulness as a full-service depot. For one thing, dockage at Lazaretto was inadequate to accommodate the growing fleet of tenders and support vessels needed in the northern Bay; most of the lighthouse service watercraft was already docked downriver, at the Curtis Bay Revenue Cutter Service Yard. Thus, Lazaretto became a construction and repair facility for many screwpile lighthouses on the Bay. Wooden, cottage-style houses for screwpiles were built at Lazaretto in "pre-fab" form and shipped by barge to the station where they were to be erected. Additionally, the iron frames of forgotten screwpiles, and even the caissons of many open-water lighthouses (still standing), were received and assembled at Lazaretto.

Eventually, the importance of the Lazaretto depot waned and, in the late 19th century, was overshadowed by construction of a new, larger depot at Portsmouth, Virginia. In addition, other depots or buoy storage facilities were placed at in-between points around the Bay: Point Lookout and Annapolis in Maryland, and even in Washington, D.C.

In the 1920s, many of the personnel at Lazaretto were transferred to Portsmouth; in 1929 the lighthouse itself was decommissioned and later, over the protests of many (including Baltimore schoolchildren), was torn down. Even so, the old depot remained a useful site for various lighthouse activities, including experiments with new fog signals and other novel equipment. In 1939, it was designated as a radio research laboratory and manufacturing facility. In fact, much of the development of radio phones and radio direction finders (RDF) took place at the Lazaretto facility.

The depot was officially closed in1958 and the land was sold to the Rukert Terminals Corporation of Baltimore. In1985, the company built a full-size replica of the light tower at Lazaretto on the terminal property.

c. 1925, Coast Guard

National Archives

The Lighthouse Board convinced the Federal government that it should transfer the vacant "fever house" adjacent to the Lazaretto station for use at the depot. Once used for small-pox victims, the brick building became the headquarters and workshop for the depot. Iron-ball anchors and concrete slab anchors for buoys are shown in the front of the building in this 1914 photo.

This color postcard, printed in Germany in 1912, shows the "Lazzerreto" station with the "fever house" behind the tower. The Naval vessel in the foreground is an unlikely customer for the depot and may be a result of it's publisher's emphasis on the coming war in Europe.

Collection of Richard Julian

A mysterious rumor persists that Edgar Allan Poe's melancholic and unfinished story, "The Lighthouse," was inspired by the stubby 30-foot Donahoo tower at Lazaretto Point. The lighthouse described, appears to be fictional, though it might draw on notes made around the Cape May or Cape Henry lights (both of which Poe must have passed on many trips between New York, New Jersey and Richmond). It is certainly a far stretch to suppose that Lazaretto Point provided descriptive material for the fragmented piece. (Of greater interest is Poe's anticipation of subterranean caisson foundations, yet to be built in the United States.)

The story is written as the log of a keeper, new to the experience and utterly alone. "Nothing to be seen, with the telescope even," the narrator begins on January 2, "but ocean and sky, with an occasional gull." On January 3 the entry reads, "A dead calm all day . . . A few sea-weeds came in sight, but besides them absolutely nothing all day--not even the slightest speck of cloud . . . Occupied myself in exploring the light-house. It is a very lofty one--as I find to my cost when I have to ascend its interminable stairs--not quite 160 feet, I should say, from the low-water mark to the top of the lantern. From the bottom inside the shaft, however, the distance to the summit is 180 feet at least--thus the floor is 20 feet below the surface of the sea, even at low-tide... It seems to me that the hollow interior at the bottom should have been filled in with solid masonry. Undoubtedly, the whole would have been thus rendered more safe . . . No mere sea . . . could accomplish anything with this solid iron-riveted wall . . ."

47

The design of the latest Upper Cedar Point and Lower Cedar Point screwpile lighthouses was virtually the same as the 1890 lighthouse at Tangier Sound and the 1889 lighthouse at Cobb Point, Maryland.

UPPER CEDAR POINT 1821-1867-1963

Upper Cedar Point light station, site of four lightships before a screwpile lighthouse was built in 1867, was a lightship station for 46 years, making it the longest serving lightship station in Maryland waters. It is not clear when each of the early ships served the station, but it is known that No. 21, the last ship on station, was a sistership to Lightship No. 24, placed at Lower Cedar Point in the same year. Lightship No. 21 served at Upper Cedar Point from 1864 until 1867 when she was moved to Willoughby Spit, Virginia, and, in 1869, she served at Wolf Trap and also temporarily, served at York Spit in late 1869. No. 21 went on to serve at Tybee Island, Georgia, and was finally retired in 1880.

The only lighthouse (shown here) to be placed at Upper Cedar Point was a square screwpile structure of the same design as the house at Lower Cedar Point. It was discontinued in 1876 when the lighthouse at Mathias Point was built 2 miles downriver, but after numerous complaints from mariners it was lighted again in 1882 and went on to serve for 71 more years. Under the Coast Guard's automation plan it was dismantled in 1963.

LOWER CEDAR POINT 1825-1867-1951

The busy Potomac River, from the Bay north to the ports of Alexandria, Virginia and Washington, was filled with dangerous shoals and narrow bends in the river. In the early 1800s, it was obvious to mariners that markers were needed for safe navigation at the "narrows," particularly at the bend at Mathias Point Neck. In 1825, the first of 2 lightships was stationed at Lower Cedar Point to protect the shallow shore on the Virginia side of the river. The ship was a small, wooden, sailing schooner showing a single light. In 1861, Confederate rebels boarded her and burned the ship beyond repair. She was replaced in 1864 by No. 24, a 77', 2-masted sailing lightship built in Massachusetts. Each mast held an iron daymarker and 2 lanterns, each having 8 oil lamps. Lightship No. 24 was withdrawn from the station in 1867, when the first screwpile lighthouse was built.

Two lighthouses served Lower Cedar Point light station. The first, a square cottage-style screwpile (of the same design as Upper Cedar Point), burned on Christmas night 1893. The assistant keeper reported it caught fire in a manner unknown to him. The second lighthouse (shown here) was put on station in 1896. It was demolished in 1951, and replaced by the light shown above supported by the original screw piles.

when Union soldiers, passing between the President Street and Camden Yard Stations, were fired upon and returned a volley of fire into the mob that had blockaded the shuttle tracks connecting the two stations and bombarded them with paving stones and rocks. There were fatalities and injuries on both sides, prompting the mayor of Baltimore City to telegraph President Lincoln imploring him to send no more troops to Baltimore. No reply was received, however, and, "the government officials . . . were left to confront this new threat on their own."[15] An emergency meeting of the town fathers calculated the risk of another clash between citizens and soldiers as high, and it was agreed the railroad bridges north of Baltimore should be destroyed.[16] Incredibly (especially from a late-twentieth century perspective which finds such locally autonomous military action difficult to conceive), the plans were indeed carried out, and officially so, by the Maryland Guard and the Baltimore City Police. Not surprisingly, the federal military presence was rapidly increased. Within days, Fort Carroll was occupied by a detachment of infantry with artillery, and, on April 27, three days after the Naval Academy's midshipmen sailed for Rhode Island on the USS *Constitution* (where the Naval Academy remained for the duration of the war), Annapolis was made headquarters of a new military department that extended, in a forty-mile band along the railroad line, all the way to Washington. On May 1, the Potomac Flotilla was established for the protection of the Bay. And, getting back to Baltimore City—before the year was out, "the mayor of Baltimore, the chief of police and the police commissioner, along with thirty-one members of the state legislature and an assortment of congressmen, judges and newspaper editors would find accommodation in Fort McHenry as a result of their political actions."[17]

Thus, the Civil War, especially the military occupation of Maryland—though one must add to this the later reopening and expansion of Virginia ports with a huge naval presence—stamped a new federal face on the Chesapeake Bay, a military one that contin-

Chesapeake Chapter, U.S. Lighthouse Society

It is known that President Lincoln's assassin, John Wilkes Booth, crossed the Potomac River near the Upper Cedar Point lighthouse, after rowing the wrong direction up Popes Creek in his failed attempt to escape.

ued to expand until fairly recent times and is still highly visible, and one that has almost certainly been influential in the disposition of many Chesapeake Bay lighthouses.

The Confederate Navy—nonexistent at the beginning of the war—was "a miracle of improvisation."[18] "Under the pressure of urgent need, the South, which had far less experience with mechanical things than the more industrialized North, suddenly became an innovator of the tools of war. In a very short time, the Confederacy was ready to send ironclads into action; it pioneered in the development of electrically exploded underwater mines and produced the first underwater craft that sank an enemy warship."[19] The first torpedoes, discovered in the Potomac in July of 1861, were examined with curiosity and defused with great care.

The North, too, had its innovations—hot air balloons that were used in aerial reconnaissance to aid the Union army in locating Confederate batteries and improving their estimate of the size and strength of Confederate troops along the Potomac that threatened the supply lines to Washington. Roads into the southern counties of Maryland, the heart of the state's Tidewater region, were few and poorly maintained. Thus, what might technically be called the first U.S. aircraft carrier—a "balloon boat"—was built to carry the reconnaissance balloons down to a position opposite Mattawoman Creek. On November 11, 1861, the first such mission was conducted

Continued on page 53

49

The BREWERTON CHANNEL RANGE
1868-1924

Mariners' Museum

LEADING POINT LIGHT-STATION.

The Brewerton Channel Range was made up of Leading Point and Hawkins Point lights on the south shore of the Patapsco River approaching Baltimore Harbor. The rear light, at Leading Point, sat on a rise of land just over a mile from the front light at Hawkins Point. Originally, the lights, built in 1868, were known only by their individual names. In 1915, when a single lightkeeper, William Raabe, became the keeper of both lights, they were renamed to honor Henry Brewerton, a Civil War engineer who worked on the defenses of Baltimore Harbor and Point Lookout.

The design of both lighthouses was unlike any others on the Bay, (except perhaps the similarity of Leading Point to the keeper's house at Sandy Point, Maryland). But Leading Point was unique with its large black ball day signal protruding from the tower roof. In the 1920s, the day marker and the light in the tower were removed and replaced by a 40' skeletal tower. Over the years, both lighthouses went through a number of different lighting and structural configurations.

Focal Plane

40'

70'

30'

Mean Low Water Level

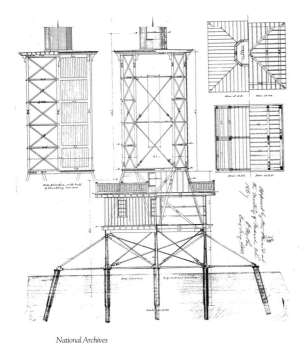

The Hawkins Point screwpile lighthouse, with its 34' tower built on top of a square (contrary to a Light List that claims it is hexagonal) was unlike any other light station on the Bay. When first built in 1868, the lighthouse had two lights; one at the top of a wood-sheathed tower at a 70' focal plane, and the other inside the building's top floor at a 28' height. The lower light was placed in one of the window frames inset into the mansard roof. Understandably, the ungainly tower above the house was not long lived, and it was torn down in the early 1900s, leaving the unusual screwpile structure to continue its function. Engineers installed a fanciful wrought iron lightning rod at the peak of the roof to enhance the roofline. The house was dismantled in 1924, and an automatic light installed on its rubble base. Both Hawkins and Leading Point lights still serve as range lights into Baltimore Harbor, albeit as simple beacons.

From 1870 until the 1960s, a U.S. Public Health quarantine station was situated at Leading Point (only a few hundred feet from the lighthouse). Upon arriving in the channel, ships from foreign ports were required to stop at the station for inspection of the passengers and crew. Known locally as the "delousing plant," the Leading Point station replaced the Lazaretto Point fever house as the port's control point for incoming diseases. The ship inspections ended in the mid-1970s (though such passenger inspections are still performed at airports).

HAWKINS' POINT
LIGHT – STATION.

Profile Section
of Land between
LEADING POINT &
HAWKINS POINT
Light Stations

Focal Plane.

28'

Mean Low Water Level

STINGRAY POINT 1858-1965
Stingray Point light was located on the south side of the entrance to the Rappahannock River, within sight of the Windmill Point light station guarding the north shore of the river's mouth. For 100 years, the hexagonal cottage remained in pristine condition, as evidenced by the 1949 photo below. Shortly after this photograph was taken, the light was automated, the lighthouse boarded up, and, in 1965, the lighthouse was dismantled.

National Archives

For 32 years, Stingray Point light was home to keeper Larry Marchant — one of the longest lightkeeping tenures on the Bay. In an interview with the *Baltimore Sun*, he stated that "the secret of my good health is that I have been where the doctors could not get me."

According to historian Arthur Pierce Middleton, 17th-century Europeans were startled and fascinated by some of the new life that they found in the Chesapeake Bay. Some encounters were painful—as was Captain John Smith's chance meeting with a stingray at the mouth of the Rappahannock River. "[H]is thigh swelled and smarted so painfully that he thought himself dying, and gave instructions to his men for the disposal of his body. Upon his recovery, Smith bestowed the name Stingray upon the nearest point of land . . . and Stingray Point retains the name until this day."

Collection, P. Hornberger

The photos of Stingray Point above and Bowlers Rock (below) were taken in 1885 by Major Jared A. Smith, 5th District Engineer based at the Lazaretto Depot. Major Smith photographed most of the lights of the Bay in the late 1800s, and he almost always placed the keeper on deck in full uniform in a jaunty pose. His photos exhibit an unusual professionalism for the time.

BOWLERS ROCK 1835-1868-1920
Bowlers Rock lighthouse was the only light station built on Virginia's Rappahannock River. It began as a lightship station in 1835 with a small 54 ton lightship, which was burned by Confederate raiders in 1861. After the Union took control of the river, Lightship No.28 was placed on station in 1864. It was an 82', 83-ton, 2-masted sailing ship built of wood at Norfolk, Virginia. She had a single lantern with 8 oil lamps and an iron hoop day marker on the mainmast. She was at Bowlers Rock for only two years before the lightship station was discontinued in 1868 upon the building of the screwpile lighthouse nearby. No.28 went on to serve as a 5th district relief vessel and later served in Galveston, Texas and was retired in 1906.

The lighthouse was a square cottage-style screwpile placed at the southern tip of an underwater rock formation in the middle of the river. The station was almost 30 miles upriver from the Bay—one of the most remote, out-of-the-way Bay lighthouses for the inspector to visit. It was subject to ice damage almost every winter and, in 1895 the Board recommended stone rubble be placed around the foundation. It survived until 1920, when it was replaced by an automatic acetylene gas light, mounted on a new base nearby.

Coast Guard

as the aircraft *Intrepid* was launched, sending one university professor (designer of the balloons) and one Union army general soaring high above the Potomac to assess the Confederate positions.[20]

For sheer disruptiveness, however, lightship tenders and lightships were attractive Confederate targets right from the beginning, occasioning skirmishes and causing disruptions right at the Union's front door. On April 18, the day after Virginia's secession, the lighthouse tender *Buchanan* was captured in the James River (in the words of the naval commander and local lighthouse inspector, he was "unexpectedly boarded . . . by a steamer from Richmond with a military company on board, and being unprepared for the attack . . . was compelled to surrender"[21]). In May, the Smith Point lightship was captured and hidden in the Great Wicomico River, but it was soon retrieved and towed back onto location—though only the first of several such incidents. Throughout the war, commanders of the ships of the Potomac Flotilla were fretted with requests for protection of the Bay's light stations. By then, both their number and their disbursement throughout the Bay and its major rivers often made for a difficult and distracting task. The orders that Flotilla commanders received often included what could almost be termed an "aside" to guard one or more of the lighthouses and lightships in the vicinity of their operations—something that was often aided by on-shore military intelligence. An order received by Lieutenant-Commander Hooker of the First Division illustrates the difficulties:

Sir: Proceed to the Rappahannock and resume your duties on that station, including within your jurisdiction the coast as far south as the Wolf Trap light-boat, to which you will be careful to give ample protection.

Send one of your boats to the Eastern shore for the protection of its lighthouses, for which purpose the commanding officer must put himself in communication with the military authorities. Do not allow the Rappahannock to be ascended higher than Urbana, and avoid all appearance of a reconnaissance of that river.[22]

Lighthouses, too, were raided during the

Coast Guard

war years, though, the fact that the keepers were members of the communities in which the lights were situated often meant that the federal property was the primary target of Confederate actions(destruction of the light and its appurtenances, confiscation of the oil and other supplies)—not the keeper and his family. A good example is Blackistone light on St. Clement's Island, raided in 1864 by a Confederate army captain and former owner of the island, John M. Goldsmith. "The Confederates smashed the lens and lamp and carried off the oil and intended to set off dynamite to blow up the building," one St. Mary's county historian notes.[23] But when the keeper protested that his wife could not be moved because she was pregnant and near term, and the wife, in turn, protested that she would accompany her husband if he were taken prisoner, the raiders relented, leaving the structure intact, the keepers unharmed. Apparently, too, as a member of a Tidewater community that traversed the banks of the Potomac, the keeper was personally known to some members of the raiding party. As in Baltimore, the ambivalence resulting from cross-cutting ties and allegiances sometimes heightened and other times assuaged the bitterness of the conflict.[24]

Southern Maryland was seen as enemy

This 1951 photo of Stingray Point lighthouse shows the placement of stone rubble around the lighthouse to break ice flows.

53

Continued on page 57

Collection P. Hornberger

WINDMILL POINT 1834-1869-1954 The light station at Windmill Point, Virginia, was located on the northern shore of the entrance to the Rappahannock River. It began with a lightship about which little is known, except that it was on station from 1834 until 1861, when it was removed by Confederate forces. Two other lightships served at Windmill Point (including a relief vessel out of Portsmouth) until 1869, when the first and only lighthouse was built. The structure was similar in design to the lighthouses built at York Spit and Smith Point, with wing-like decks extending from two sides of the house. The larger decks allowed for more storage and better support for heavy fog machinery. The house was constructed at the Lazaretto Depot in Baltimore and shipped on 2 schooners to the site some 120 miles down the Bay.

The 1952 interior layout shown here is a later configuration designed to accommodate a crew of 5 Coast Guardsmen. The lighthouse was discontinued in 1954 and dismantled in 1965 during the Coast Guard's modernization program.

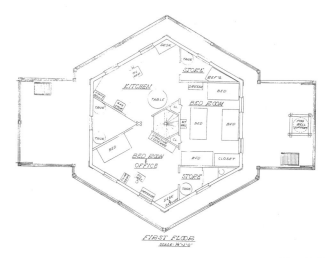

FIRST FLOOR

National Archives

Coast Guard

In the summer of 1940, the lighthouse was witness to the dismasting of the schooner, *Fannie Isley*, on her way to Crisfield with a load of oyster shells. The schooner's seams opened and she sank in 50' of water, just north of the lighthouse. Such events were frequent near Bay lighthouses, but usually only recorded in the keeper's log—and, unless it involved the lighthouse, of little interest to the Board.

This very "yachty" looking crew (notice the feathered hat, forward) made up of guests from the Tides Inn Hotel is heading out to see the lighthouse aboard the hotel's 83' yacht, the *Suntan*, which entertained guests in the early 1950s. The Irvington, Virginia hotel now has a much larger yacht. Alas, no lighthouse is now within an afternoon cruise of the hotel.

Windmill Lighthouse

Aboard The "Sun Tan" Tides Inn Irvington, Va.

Collection, Herb Entwistle

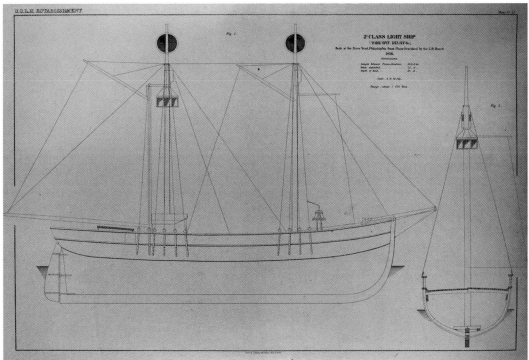

The first lightship at York Spit station (later designated "T") was an 81'6" schooner-rigged vessel built in 1856 by the Philadelphia Navy Yard from plans submitted by the Lighthouse Board. One of the earliest attempts to build vessels specifically for lightship service, she was heavily built of white oak planking with copper and iron fastenings. Her broad beam of 21'6" and draft of 10'6" was designed to prevent the roll and pitch usually found in standard sailing ships while at anchor. But the ship had no engine and was therefore difficult to keep on station in bad weather. She had accommodations for a captain and a crew of 8. The lantern, with 8 oil lamps and reflectors, was raised each evening on the rear mast. At each masthead was an iron hoop daymarker. Like other early lightships she had a 22" diameter fog bell forward, which had to be hand-struck for hours during heavy weather.

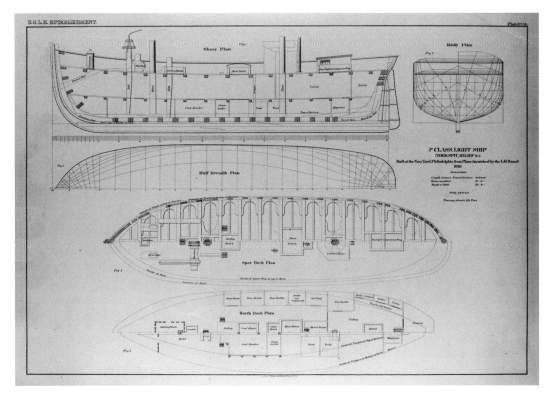

YORK SPIT 1856-1869-1960 York Spit station stood in 12 ' of water at the entrance to Virginia's York River. It stood as a clear guide for shipping up and down the Bay between New Point Comfort lighthouse and the light at Back River, and also served as the mark into the York River. The York Spit station was first served by the lightship later designated "T," shown on the previous page. "T" was removed from her station in 1861 by Confederate forces. Lightship No.12, a 72' ship that had been at Wolf Trap station, was placed at York Spit from 1863 to 1864. Lightship No.21, a 78' ship, was placed on station temporarily while the screwpile lighthouse was being built in1869.

The lighthouse was similar in design to the lighthouse at Windmill Point (and the first lighthouse at Wolf Trap) with its two extended decks. Its base was sitting on 14 iron-encased wooden pilings, driven at great effort into a very hard bottom. An enclosed tower, looking something like a mini-lighthouse, was constructed on the edge of one of the decks in1886 and placed on top of the existing fog bell apparatus. In 1933, after a severe summer storm, York Spit keeper W. J. Diggs succinctly reported, "Floors began to

burst up. Sailboat broke away. Sea breaking over deck. Oil tanks broke away." Finding the keeper's boat ashore, it was at first assumed Diggs had drowned, but he had been taken off the lighthouse earlier by a passing fisherman. After almost 100 years of service, the lighthouse at York Spit became another project of Coast Guard modernization and in the summer of 1960, the light was automated and the structure dismantled.

territory by the Union forces—indeed, its people performed valuable services for the Confederacy—and here (for example, at Blackistone and Point Lookout lights) as elsewhere in the South, the lighthouses were placed under military guard and protected by gunboat. Nevertheless, the Potomac blockade was unable to contain the steady flow of people and goods between the Virginia and southern Maryland shores. "Marylanders rowed across the river even when the moon was full, and ran the blockade in sloops and yawls."[25]

In spite of the Civil War, the 1850s and late 1860s were busy years of lighthouse construction on the Chesapeake Bay. In Maryland, the "lost lighthouses" from this period include Blackistone Island, Janes Island, and, for all practical purposes, Fort Carroll, as well as the Brewerton Channel Range (Hawkins Point and Leading Point), Somers Cove, Upper Cedar Point and Lower Cedar Point. From the same period Virginia has lost an equal number of lighthouses, including Pungoteague River, Jordan Point, Deep Water Shoals, Point of Shoals and White Shoals, Stingray Point, Bowlers Rock and Windmill Point. By 1870, eight lightships had been removed from the Chesapeake and its tributaries, leaving (except the Choptank River lightship, 1870-1871, never a formally designated lightship station) only the relatively open-water stations at Smith Point and Wolf Trap, and these not for long. In their place were trim clapboard dwellings with rooftop lanterns outfitted with the latest French-cut lenses and showing a brilliant, and much more reliable light. These were the halcyon days of quaint lighthouses on the Bay, a time faintly recalled and longingly traced in memories of those who grew up close to one of the old lighthouses. By the end of the 1960s, most of these lighthouses were gone.

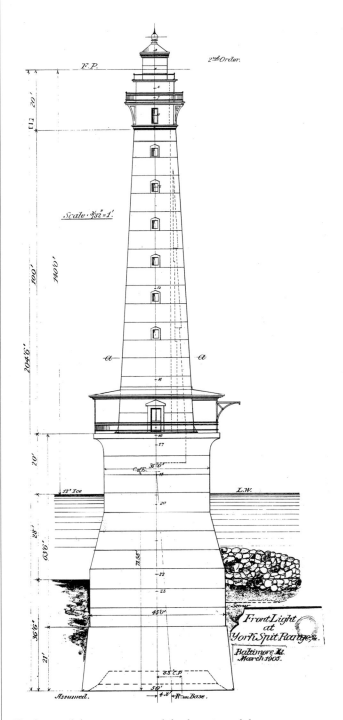

Evidence of the importance of the location of the station at York Spit is shown here in this 1905 plan for the front light of the proposed York Spit Range. The brick caisson tower would have been 140' from low water to focal plane of the light, making it only 53' shorter than the largest U.S. brick lighthouse at Cape Hatteras, North Carolina. The rear range light was to be a caisson steel tower 170' tall. Neither light was built—for what, at the time, were probably sound financial considerations.

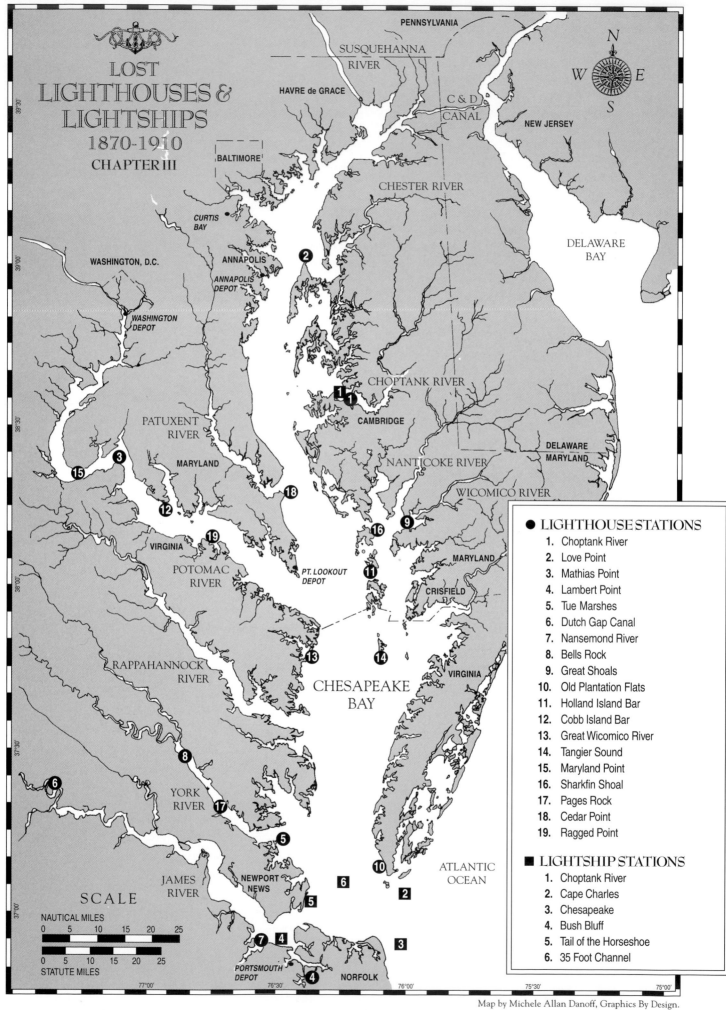

LOST LIGHTHOUSES & LIGHTSHIPS
1870-1910
CHAPTER III

PENNSYLVANIA

SUSQUEHANNA RIVER

HAVRE de GRACE

C & D CANAL

NEW JERSEY

BALTIMORE

CHESTER RIVER

DELAWARE BAY

CURTIS BAY

WASHINGTON, D.C.

ANNAPOLIS

ANNAPOLIS DEPOT

WASHINGTON DEPOT

CHOPTANK RIVER

CAMBRIDGE

PATUXENT RIVER

MARYLAND

NANTICOKE RIVER

DELAWARE
MARYLAND

WICOMICO RIVER

VIRGINIA

POTOMAC RIVER

MARYLAND

CRISFIELD

PT. LOOKOUT DEPOT

RAPPAHANNOCK RIVER

VIRGINIA

CHESAPEAKE BAY

YORK RIVER

JAMES RIVER

NEWPORT NEWS

ATLANTIC OCEAN

SCALE

NAUTICAL MILES
0   5   10   15   20   25

STATUTE MILES
0   5   10   15   20   25

PORTSMOUTH DEPOT

NORFOLK

● LIGHTHOUSE STATIONS
1. Choptank River
2. Love Point
3. Mathias Point
4. Lambert Point
5. Tue Marshes
6. Dutch Gap Canal
7. Nansemond River
8. Bells Rock
9. Great Shoals
10. Old Plantation Flats
11. Holland Island Bar
12. Cobb Island Bar
13. Great Wicomico River
14. Tangier Sound
15. Maryland Point
16. Sharkfin Shoal
17. Pages Rock
18. Cedar Point
19. Ragged Point

■ LIGHTSHIP STATIONS
1. Choptank River
2. Cape Charles
3. Chesapeake
4. Bush Bluff
5. Tail of the Horseshoe
6. 35 Foot Channel

Map by Michele Allan Danoff, Graphics By Design.

CHAPTER III

In the 1870s and 1880s, the boom years of lighthouse construction on the Chesapeake Bay continued—even, it might be said, accelerated, slowing down in the 1890s and virtually coming to a halt in the first years of the twentieth century. Many new lights were commissioned—by far the greatest number of screwpile design, comparatively easy to assemble and to anchor in shoals and muddy river bottoms. Because the screwpile light was also relatively inexpensive, there was little resistance to the establishment of additional light stations on the heavily trafficked Bay. These years also saw the construction of many open-water caissons on the Chesapeake, lighthouses that survive (usually as active navigational aids) to the present, though generally greatly deteriorated since their automation. Except for the difficulties encountered in the variable substratum of the Bay, requiring the pneumatic sinking of some of the caisson structures (with all the dangers that attended to sending workmen thirty or more feet below the mud or hard shoals of the bottom), the Bay did not present the kind of engineering challenges in lighthouse design and construction that the Board was facing on the Pacific coast or on the Great Lakes. During this period, the shipping lanes to Baltimore were deepened and widened, and two new sets of range lights—the Craighill Channel and the Cutoff Channel lights—shortened the approach.

In the last quarter of the nineteenth century, the reassuring presence of lightkeepers and their families was deeply ingrained in the day-to-day life of all who lived along the Chesapeake Bay, a remembered part of the experience of everyone who ever set sail, dropped anchor or booked passage on one of the steamers that plied its waters from port to port—and there were many. The people of the Chesapeake were familiar "with the contours of the land or the meandering lines of creeks and inlets, rivers and the Bay itself. Most travel was by water, even as stage roads were improved and, later still, as trains extended their rails along some of the major routes between Washington and Richmond . . .. The people of the tidewater were cosmopolitan in a sense that goes far beyond the experience of contemporary city-dwellers. Not only were they transportation experts...but they were, and always had been, part of an international economy."[1]

In these years, however, the job of lighthouse keeper was qualitatively changed as the Lighthouse Board evidenced more concern with the regulation of the keeper's activities, setting new standards and extending its management into a variety of tasks—and even attitudes—that did not directly pertain to the showing of a good light or general upkeep of the station. The extra demands, however, did not signal any substantial benefits for the keepers; in spite of its detailed study of the lighthouse personnel systems of England and France, the Lighthouse Board still did not support a pension for their employees, something that the European lightkeepers already enjoyed and something for which the Board received criticism from some quarters. "It is to be hoped that civil service reform will make its way into this department of government," one observer wrote in the mid-1870s, lamenting that politics still had a role to play in the hiring and firing of keepers, and noting that "[i]n England the light-keeper holds his office for life or good behavior."[2] More than fifteen years later, one Board member noted that as yet "no attempt" had been made "to pension those who become maimed or worn out in its service"[3]—blunt wording that suggests the author himself did not approve. Finally, in May of 1896, civil service classifica-

The 1870s could be called the Golden Age of lighthouse keeping on the Chesapeake Bay.

A lighthouse tender crew (including mascot on second officer's lap) in full uniform. Seamen have always carried animals on board ships and the recvords indiacte no objection from the Lighthouse Board.

tion was extended to the lighthouse service, though the benefits to lightkeepers were minimal—they did not, for example, include any form of disability retirement, or, even, a salary increase.

In every way, there was greater emphasis on hierarchy, ceremony and discipline; flags had been adopted for all parts of the service, and keepers were required to purchase and wear uniforms and regulation work clothes for maintenance chores around the station. "Keepers and assistant keepers of light-stations will wear the prescribed uniform at all times," instructions now specified, "except that the coat will be taken off and the regulation apron worn when at work cleaning, and the prescribed brown working-suit will be worn when at ordinary out-door work."[4] The same rules held for the masters, mates and crews of lightships.

By the 1890s, the entire service was in uniform (except women, substitutes and temporary employees) and a Board member ob-

served, with an up-to-date flourish of French, that "it adds much to the appearance of the personnel, and does much to raise the esprit de corps, and to preserve its discipline," though he shortly added his own observation that "[t]he discipline of the Service is somewhat rigid and severe . . .."[5]

Of course, the keeper was still cautioned to exercise the strictest economy in the care and use of all supplies and was held personally responsible for every item of government property. Anything improperly receipted, improperly examined upon delivery (and later found unacceptable) and anything unaccounted for was chargeable against the keeper's salary—in the Board's words, "keepers shall be held pecuniarily responsible for all for which they receipt."[6] All of the property used at light stations was required to be of Lighthouse Board issue, including such small items as matches.

Increasing stress was laid upon paperwork: besides the detailed monthly reports to the inspector and engineer, the quarterly returns that were transmitted to the inspector three times a year, and, at the close of the fiscal year, the annual returns of the light station—all prepared in duplicate by the keeper—there were new "named" reports, including monthly fog-signal and absence reports, salary vouchers, receipts for supplies, and "unusual occurrence" and "shipwreck" reports, now formally requested. Daily expenditure and general account books were kept at all stations, along with a daily journal and a watch book. Keepers were also expected to be ready to act as public relations agents for the Lighthouse Board—to be "courteous and polite to all visitors," to "show them everything of interest about the station at such times as will not interfere with lighthouse duties."[7] (Actually, this aspect of the keeper's job owed much to tradition; even Pleasonton had expected as much.)

The growing emphasis upon formality and ceremony as a necessary component of the lightkeeper's duties was manifested in other ways besides buttons, braids and chinstraps; for example, upon their approach and departure from the lighthouse station, lighthouse and government vessels were now to be saluted with three strokes of the station's bell—as were any vessels "known by the keeper to have on board any person entitled to the courtesy of a salute."[8] On lighthouse vessels, service flags let a keeper know if the inspector, or possibly even a member of the Board, was approaching his watch. "The salute," the instructions note, "will be returned by three blasts of the whistle or by three strokes of the bell."[9]

Thus, by the latter years of the nineteenth century, the Board's authority was strongly present in many details of the keeper's daily life. "Utmost neatness of buildings and premises" was demanded and was extended into privy quarters: "Bedrooms, as well as other parts of the dwelling," the Board warned, "must be neatly kept. Untidiness will be strongly reprehended, and its continuance will subject a keeper to dismissal."[10] Though no specific mention is made of wives in connection with the performance of household

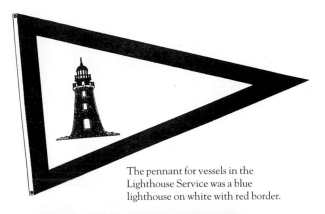

The pennant for vessels in the Lighthouse Service was a blue lighthouse on white with red border.

Flag of the Commissioner of Lighthouses

Lighthouse Service badge

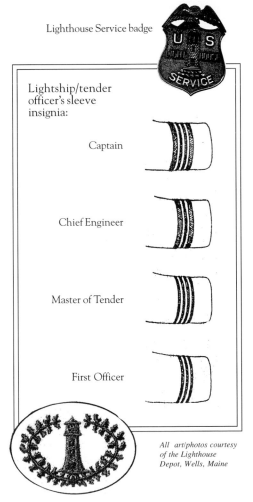

Lightship/tender officer's sleeve insignia:

Captain

Chief Engineer

Master of Tender

First Officer

All art/photos courtesy of the Lighthouse Depot, Wells, Maine

Cap ornament

61

In the 1902 publication *Instructions to Lightkeepers and Masters of Lighthouse Vessels* under "Instructions for Painting," was the following regulation:

Regulation #305. "The following colors only shall be used in the painting of lighthouse structures:"

OUTSIDE COLORS

Dark red .... } For wooden structures
Brown or white ....

Red or lead color ...... For trimmings of structures

Black   For lanterns and gallery railings

Brown .... For iron structures, and to replace black on the outside of all structures

Red, green or brown ....For outside shutters

Red .... In exceptional cases, to mark the starboard side in entering channels

Whitewash............... On stone and brick where a change in natural color is authorized and on rough board work

INSIDE COLORS

White ..... For the interior of lanterns, generally for all woodwork, except hardwood

Green .....For pedestals and service tables

Lead color ...For floors, staircases and walls when authorized to be painted. Hard pine floors and hard woods are not to be painted, but shall be kept well oiled and scrubbed

Black ... For iron staircases and railings, and for interior ironwork in general

Black or white ...For underside of tower stairways
Whitewash ....For walls, cellars, and outhouses and rough board work when painting has not been authorized

Whitewash .... For walls, cellars, and outhouses and rough board work when painting has not been authorized

chores, the incursion of Board regulations into the private household of the keeper and his family may have reinforced the growing distinctions between men and women at lighthouse stations. Even though during this period some women managed to obtain or hold onto their jobs as keepers, the fact that there were no uniforms for women also suggested that their status and participation was regarded as qualitatively different—and perhaps (like that of substitutes and temporary help) was not expected to last.

By the end of this period on the Chesapeake Bay, women and children had been removed from residence on many light stations. Now they lived in the communities close at hand with only a brief sojourn on the lighthouse with their children during the summer months. There were ready justifications for the exclusion of women and children (just as at an earlier time Pleasonton had found in the excellent training received as

lightkeeper's wife an excellent justification for the hiring of women). Most of the new rationale had reference to the changes made in fog signals, especially the heavy machinery that the new signals required—for example, the boilers for steam-operated whistles and the heavily weighted winding mechanisms for 1,000-pound fog bells. Assistant keepers were formally assigned to these stations, but it was now believed they should be men, preferably men with a good deal of mechanical experience. The work of stoking a boiler, for example, was both physically taxing and potentially dangerous. On the Chesapeake Bay, there was also the considerable danger of large fields of moving ice—a proven threat to screwpile structures in the winter months.

Besides the dangers of winter ice (which prompted some keepers to move their wives and children to shore, irrespective of the Board's wishes) the switch to kerosene probably also contributed to the estimation of

danger to women and children at some of the Bay's lighthouses. Kerosene, as the Board noted in 1877, was an illuminant "not unattended with danger."[11] In fact, the substitution of this far more economical oil was slow in coming, for the Board first sought "a thorough acquaintance with the nature of the substance" and conducted numerous experiments over a period of several years "with the different varieties of this material found in the market."[12] At the same time, they studied the best means to test batches of the explosive substance from different suppliers, ways to store, transport and preserve it on station, and the proper methods to instruct the keepers in its use. Kerosene was fearsome. "The kind generally employed," they reported, "gives off a vapor, which, when mingled in a certain proportion with atmospheric air, is capable of exploding with the violence of gunpowder; and the material itself, when once kindled burns with an en-

ergy almost incontrollable."[13] Initially, kerosene was introduced in specially designed lamps for fourth, fifth and sixth-order lights—the size of most of the Bay's lights. Twice as much storage room was required as had been for lard oil, which must have made a significant cut in the space allotment on the small screwpile lighthouses. For safety reasons, the Board was soon insisting that money be appropriated for separate oil houses at all shore-based stations—obviously, however, such an arrangement was not generally possible for the open-water lighthouses.

All in all, the lighthouse service clearly experienced many of the same distinctions and divisions in the assignment of chores to men and women that accompanied industrialization throughout American society (and experienced them early on). It seems worthwhile to consider the ways in which the recognition of the keeper's wife, and her role in keeping the light, was formally discouraged

Lighthouse keeper
in regulation
uniform
winds a fog
bell signal

Keeper's
collar insignia

63

c. 1901, Collection P. Hornberger

The schooner, *Lewis Jane,* in Baltimore Harbor loaded with the prefabricated sections needed to build the Hoopers Island lighthouse.

and informally disavowed, for it was not too many years later that the men themselves were deemed superfluous in the operation of a good light—this final shift, one might say, to robotics. Even in the 1870s, the enthusiasm for machinery, its precision and perfect discipline (at least when it was working) inspired a kind of excited admiration.

Nevertheless, where husband and wife occupied a screwpile cottage on the Bay in the twentieth century, there still were instances of the wife's formal appointment as assistant keeper who took, in her husband's absence, full responsibility for the light—and, it is worth noting, that wives still learned all the skills necessary to manage a light. In fact, wives were relied upon by the lighthouse service although they could no longer look forward to appointment as full keepers in the event of their husband's death.

With one exception—a four hundred-ton "iron boat" placed on Louisiana shoals in 1847—all lightships were constructed of wood until 1882. Interestingly, there seems to have been more resistance to the introduction of metal hulls in lightship construction than elsewhere in shipbuilding, and there were probably several reasons for this resistance, some of them already alluded to: first, the shipbuilders' interests and the traditional crafts they represented; second, the belief that wood was superior in tensile strength and resilience—critical for ships that were moored in one spot and subjected to extreme punishment by wind and wave; and third, the belief that wooden ships offered a healthier environment. But perhaps of greatest importance during the 1860s and 1870s is the fact that relatively little was yet known about the preservation of metal daily exposed to the corrosive power of salt water. When the change to iron and steel finally came, it was decisive. Beginning with Lightship No. 44, all light vessels were built of iron and steel. Other improvements also now came to fruition: the bilge keel, giving the ship greater stability, and self-propulsion. Even so, replacement was

64

slow. The typical late nineteenth century lightship was a strongly built, two-masted schooner, showing colored disks as a day mark, and, by night, powerful lights consisting of eight or nine lamps with reflectors suspended on gimbals so that the beam of light would project horizontally, irrespective of the motion of the ship.[14]

For eighteen years following the removal of Lightship No. 22 from Wolf Trap Shoal (No. 22 was one of five lightships built at New Bedford, Massachusetts during the Civil War), there was no lightship on the Chesapeake Bay. Then, in 1888, a station was established at Cape Charles. Others soon followed at Bush Bluff and Tail of the Horseshoe, requiring the acquisition and outfitting of the necessary relief vessels. Interestingly, in addition to the eighty-seven ton schooner *Drift*, the lighthouse tender *Holly* was outfitted briefly to serve as relief vessel at Bush Bluff station. Emergencies were often the result of severe winter ice in the Chesapeake Bay. The winter of 1895 provides a good example. On

February 15, the Bush Bluff light vessel was carried away by heavy ice. The schooner *Drift* was placed on station three days later and on March 5, the *Drift* was relieved by the side-wheel tender *Holly*. Meanwhile, Lightship No. 46 had been sent to Smith Point, Virginia, "in the place," the Board reported, "of the Smith Point light-house which was carried away by ice Feb. 14 . . .. Before going on this station, two quick steaming boilers were installed and certain general repairs were made. She is efficient and kept in good condition."[15]

In 1895, Lightship No. 49 was also in good condition on the Cape Charles station. Like No. 46, this ship did long service on the Bay—in fact, both ships remained on the Bay until 1923, when they were described in an annual report of the Bureau of Lighthouses (though changes in illuminant and fog signal had been made to No. 49). In 1922, No. 46 was removed from the Tail of the Horseshoe station—replaced by a new gas buoy with an acetylene gas light and gas-operated fog bell. In its very first year, the buoy, which cost

Ice in Baltimore harbor soon after the massive fire of 1904. Ice movement on the Bay was the natural enemy of screwpile lighthouses.

Continued on page 91

65

Mariners' Museum

PORTSMOUTH DEPOT 1870

In 1870, the Portsmouth Depot was established to rectify a long-standing problem: the deficiency of storage for buoys and coal, and the lack of berthing for lightships and tenders in the lower Bay. A large lot was purchased and enclosed with a board fence, a wharf was built, and skids were made where the huge iron buoys could be laid for repair. The buoy depot was in full working order by 1872 and proved extremely useful. Two years later, the Lighthouse Board reported that, besides the storing of spare buoys, emergency supplies and the tons of coal consumed by the tenders and lighthouse stations, the depot had become the place of manufacture for most of the spar buoys used in the 5th District.

Over the next few years, however, difficulties with adjoining property owners curtailed the growing utility of the facility. For reasons not mentioned in the Board's reports, the owners would not permit use of the depot slip on their side of the wharf and, finding it impossible to negotiate a purchase or to condemn some of the privately held land, the Board decided to move the expanding depot to Fort Monroe. Soundings were obtained along the frontage of land set aside by the War Department. The Board was confident that a solution had been found: "An appropriation of $10,000 is needed for the

Today, the Coast Guard maintains a primary facility in Portsmouth, and the surrounding Hampton Roads area. Portsmouth is the headquarters of the 5th Coast Guard District and the Command Office of the Atlantic Area, which includes 4 other Districts. The tenders *Red Cedar*, *Chock*, and *Kennebec* are homeported in Portsmouth, along with the cutters, helicopters and aircraft of the 5th District. Portsmouth headquarters manages small boat stations at Chincoteague, Wachapreague, Hudgins, Norfolk and Cape Charles, Virginia, as well as the tenders and stations in Maryland.

c.1880, National Archives

erection of the wharf and sheds to enable the Board to establish an excellent, roomy, and well-placed depot, after which the old site at Portsmouth can be sold for more than the sum required to put the new depot on a proper footing." But the following year, new soundings showed a remarkable difference, proving "that the site near Fort Monroe was unsuitable...." Repairs were made at the Portsmouth Depot and the old problems with neighbors continued, though activities at the depot also continued to expand.

In the 1920s, the Bureau of Lighthouses was still complaining of the need to acquire a 35'-wide strip of adjacent land. The land, it was explained, belonged to the Seaboard Wharf & Warehouse Company which, according to Commissioner Putnam, allowed their side of the wharf to deteriorate so badly that the entire wharf was useless. By now, there were small depots up and down the Bay, but Portsmouth was clearly the ideal location for 5th District headquarters; there was no chance of expanding the facility at Baltimore and, clearly, the Lighthouse Bureau hoped to move headquarters to a more central location. Once again, the War Department offered land; once again, it was rejected—very likely after the adjacent property owners received and accepted a reasonable proposal for purchase of adjoining land. Beginning in 1926, appropriations were finally received to modernize and enlarge the depot. Renovations and building went on until 1932 when 5th District headquarters was finally transferred to Portsmouth—where, in fact, it remains to the present day.

Nearby forests of Virginia pine supplied the Portsmouth Depot with abundant raw material to fabricate almost all the Bay's spar buoys. Spar buoys are seen neatly stacked in front of the depot headquarters building shown above.

Portsmouth Depot was home port to the lightships of 5th District, including the 132' lightship *Winter-Quarter*, which served 13 miles off the Atlantic coast at Assateague Island. Although she was never used in the Chesapeake, she marked the approach to the Bay for ships from the north.

CHOPTANK RIVER 1870-1871-1964 This station was located inside the Choptank River at Benoni Point, marking the entrance to the Tred Avon River into Oxford and guiding boats between Castle Haven Point and Chlora Point. It was first served by Lightship No.25, a 61' schooner-rigged ship with a single lantern. No.25 had already served as the lightship at Hooper Strait station from 1827 until 1867 and three more years as relief ship during the building of Deepwater Shoals. She was assigned to the Choptank station in 1870 to be a temporary light while the lighthouse was being built. This first Choptank River lighthouse was of cottage design, similar to the lighthouse recently built at York Spit, Virginia, including its use of wooden piles encased in cast-iron sleeves. It lasted until 1917, when a large ice flow destroyed the structure leading the Board to review plans for a replacement including a unique plan (opposite) for placing the existing cottage-style structure on a new cement filled caisson base. The costly proposed plan was rejected with the Board electing instead to use the spare Cherrystone lighthouse still in storage at Cape Charles, Virginia.

The Cherrystone lighthouse was moved to the Choptank station in 1921, ten years after the last screwpile lighthouse at Ragged Point, Virginia was built. It lasted for another 43 years, serving the numerous waterman and the continually increasing pleasure boat traffic in the area. It was demolished in 1964.

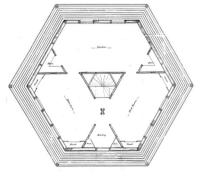

Interior layout of Choptank/Cherrsytone lighthouse. c. 1885

LOVE POINT 1872-1964 Love Point lies on the northern most tip of Kent Island on Maryland's Eastern Shore. The lighthouse stood on the shallow shoal extending one-half mile from the point that once held two large hotels and a bayside boardwalk. The aptly named *Smokey Joe*, a sooty steam ferry from Baltimore, dropped summer vacationers off at the popular Love Point Hotel and other resorts during the 1900s. After WWII, most of the beach facilities had closed and boat passenger traffic stopped running to the Point.

The lighthouse was built by Francis A. Gibbons, the same builder of the first lighthouse at Choptank River (and other lighthouses in Florida and North Carolina). Baltimorean Gibbons and his partner, Francis Kelly, apparently in good standing with Fifth Auditor Pleasanton, also built the first 8 lighthouses on the West Coast of the United States. Unfortunately, Gibbons and Kelly's extensive building record nationally is somewhat overshadowed by the regional fame of John Donahoo.

The Love Point lighthouse was a hexagonal cottage-style screwpile structure with brown pilings, red roof and white house, which showed an unusually powerful three-and-one-half order lens. The lighthouse was built in August of 1872, and that very first winter the light had to be extinguished and the keeper removed when ice flows severed some of its pilings. Winter storms often threatened Love Point, as is evident in the 1902 photo below. The lighthouse was automated in 1953 and finally demolished in 1964.

The tender *Holly* can be seen steaming in the background of the snow-bound Love Point lighthouse in 1902

LAMBERT POINT 1872-1892 Ships entering the busy Elizabeth River at Norfolk, Virginia in a fog would often run aground on the shoal at Lambert Point. In 1872 a small lighthouse was built on 5 piles instead of the planned 6 to make use of some piles that "were on hand." It was designed along the lines of the square lighthouse at White Shoals on the James River, except it was painted dark brown. A few months after it was completed, the house settled about 14" on one side due to unequal distribution of supplies and the soft character of the bottom. Using common sense, the engineers lowered the remaining 4 piles to an equal level and secured all of them with an extra piling. Later, the engineers drove more pilings and built a dock-like structure around the house in an effort to stem the structure's movement.

In 1885, the Norfolk and Western Railroad built a large coal wharf next to the lighthouse. Unfortunately, dredging for the wharf caused the lighthouse to settle again, this time by 6 inches. By now, so much industrial construction around the lighthouse had occurred that it was difficult for mariners to see the light in any case. In the meantime, the house was still settling and, fearful that any more movement of the structure would set it on fire, the Board decided to discontinue the light station in 1892. In response to mariner's complaints about the lack of protection against the constant fog in the area, the Board re-established the fog bell signal in 1901 on the lantern gallery of the old tilted house. The fog bell operated for another 10 or so years until the building collapsed.

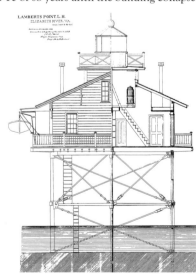

The larger boat on davits is the Coast Guard's 25', gas-powered, single-screw launch issued to many Bay lighthouses in the 1940s.

TUE MARSHES 1875-1960 Formerly known as Too's Marshes, this lighthouse was located one-half mile out from Tue Point on the Roast Meat Flats on the south side of the mouth of the York River. It was a square screwpile, cottage-style house, similar to the lighthouse at Great Shoals, except for its more intricate woodwork railings and trim. Notice how the railings have been minimized in later years for ease of maintenance. The lighthouse was automated in 1960 and demolished soon after. It was replaced by a light on its old foundation

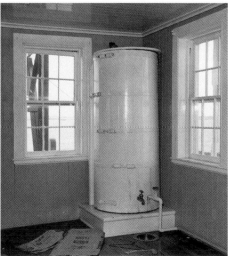

Oak water tanks in most screwpile lighthouses such as this one at Tue Marshes were fed by rainwater running from the roof. When it looked like rain was coming, the keeper would rush to scrub the roof. The water tank was cleaned almost every time it was empty.

The canal at Dutch
Gap was located at
an extreme loop in
the upper James
River, creating
Farrar's Island.

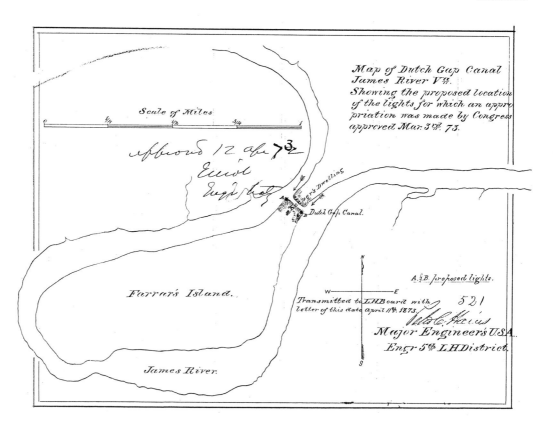

National Archives

The keeper's house was a pleasant clapboard structure, but it was built much too close to the cliff overlooking the river and had to be moved back on rollers.

DUTCH GAP CANAL 1875-1910
The Dutch Gap light is the last station going up the James River toward Richmond. The canal was dug by Union troops in 1864 as a way of permitting Federal gunboats to proceed upriver to the Confederate defenses of Richmond. Under continous fire from rebel sharpshooters and artillery, Union troops dug nearly 67,000 cubic yards of soil to open 174 yards of canal. General U.S. Grant was invited to witness the final explosion needed to open the north end of the canal. He declined, fortunately. The blast, fueled by a 12,000- pound charge of powder, threw tons of dirt right back into the freshly dug ditch. It was April 1865 and the digging of the canal was much too late to be of any value to the war effort and the project was abandoned.

It wasn't until 1871 that the canal was improved and dredged. The finished canal was able to cut almost 5 miles off the loop around Farrar Island, but it needed a light station with lights at both entrances of the cut. Two 27' post lanterns were put at river level at each entrance and a comfortable keeper's house was built on the cliff above. The lights did not require great brilliancy and small lanterns burning mineral oil were used. Flooding was a frequent problem at the station, carrying the lamp posts downriver. As a result, two supporting posts were constructed at the Lazaretto Depot.

The cliff by the keeper's house was eroding, and in 1890 the house was put on rollers and moved 130' from the cliff's edge. A new kitchen was added and the total station was repaired with a new a cistern and outhouses. The station operated until about 1910 when the lights were replaced by fixed canal lights. The keeper's house was at first rented to a local family, but eventually fell into disrepair and was soon demolished.

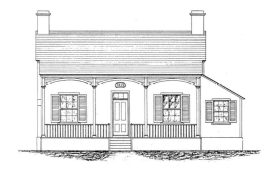

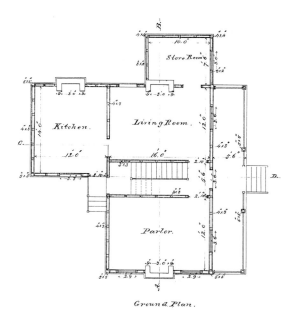

Ground Plan.

73

MATHIAS POINT 1876-1963 Mathias Point station was placed at the edge of a shoal jutting out from the major bend in the Potomac River, some 50 miles from the Bay. The point was considered one of the most dangerous navigation problems on the river. In 1872, the Board requested funds to build a lighthouse upriver at Shipping Point at the mouth of Quantico Creek, apparently responding to pressure from the Richmond, Fredericksburg & Potomac Railroad to help their ferry operations at Quantico. But the District inspector and engineer concluded that a light at Mathias Point and another at Port Tobacco would better serve mariners. In 1874, after further consideration (and a limited appropriation), the Board decided to build the Tobacco Flats lighthouse only and

install a day beacon at Mathias Point. Plans drawn by the Lighthouse Board exist for the proposed screwpile lighthouse at Tobacco Flats and an identical lighthouse at Thomas Point, near Annapolis. The lighthouse at Thomas Point was soon built but, instead of a house, Tobacco Flats got a day beacon, and the lighthouse shown here was built at Mathias Point.

New plans were drawn up for Mathias Point and the result was a lighthouse like no other screwpile on the Bay. The design of Mathias Point included 3 well-proportioned levels unlike most of the 2-level, cottage-style lighthouses on the Bay. In addition, it had an unusual amount of intricate detailed woodwork. There were no dormer windows. Instead, the hexagonal second level held 6 windows. The pilings were angled inward to the base of the lighthouse. The house was white, the roof was brown and the shutters were green. The 5th-order lens was lit just before Christmas, 1876. In 1951, the light was automated and in a dual responsibility, keeper John C. Lewis from Maryland Point lighthouse was assigned to also watch over Mathias Point. In 1963, the beautiful lighthouse at Mathias Point was demolished.

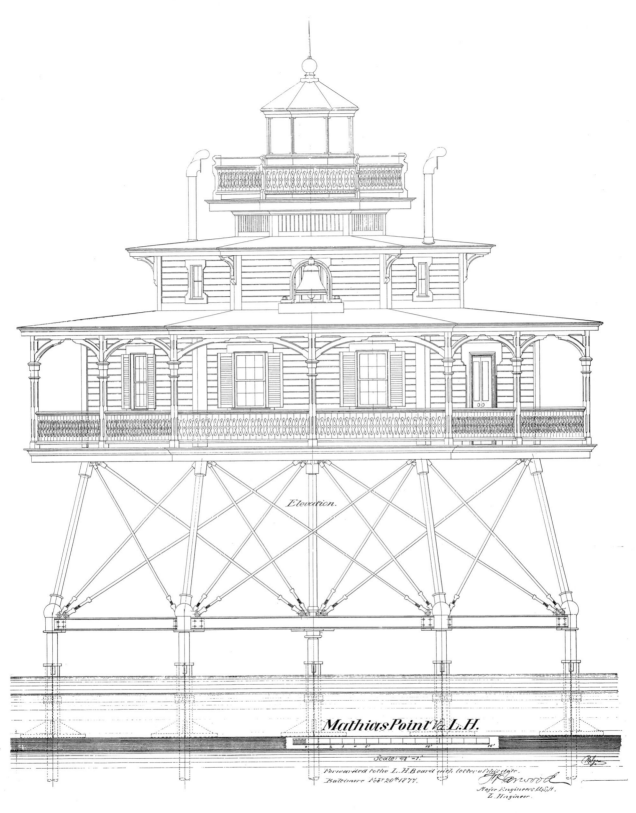

Elevation.

Mathias Point Va L.H.

Scale: ⅜'' = 1'.

Forwarded to the L.H. Board with letter of this date.
Baltimore Feb 20th 1877.

J. Kenwood
Major Engineers U.S.A.
L. Engineer.

The lighthouse at Mathias Point is the only screwpile cottage style lighthouse to be designed with a large second floor and smaller third floor level resulting in a pleasing "wedding cake" profile. The design for the structure was one -of-a-kind and, unlike many other screwpile designs, no reference was made on the plans to duplicate the design for any other structure.

POINT LOOKOUT DEPOT 1883-1965 The Point Lookout Buoy Depot was established in 1883 on property adjacent to the lighthouse proper. Both the Lazaretto and Portsmouth facilities were hemmed in and the considerable length of the Bay, as well as the inclusion of the North Carolina coasts and rivers in the 5th District, meant that location of the District's headquarters in Baltimore created a serious logistical problem. Point Lookout was midway between the two larger facilities and, conveniently as well, at the mouth of the Potomac River.

A 64' by 30' wharf was constructed and 100 metal-sheathed pine piles were driven, extending the slip about 250 feet into the water. A large buoy shed, set upon brick piers and walls, was also constructed—its interior raised above the high-water mark and paved with brick. In 1884, a large coal shed was added to the existing structure and similarly raised and paved in brick. A tramway led from both buildings to the wharf. Car wheels and axles were purchased and 2 cars were made for the tramway along with 9 sets of buoy skids. A few years later, a 5000-gallon cedar water tank was built in the buoy shed to supply tenders with fresh water. A room was built around it for protection against weather and dust. Gutters and downspouts were placed on both the coal and buoy sheds to carry rainwater into the tank.

The depot was nonetheless threatened by high water, and when, in 1888, the shoreline encroached upon one of the buildings, a breakwater became necessary—the first, constructed with nothing more than damaged cement received from nearby Fort Washington. In the 1890s, a new wharf was built with metal-sheathed oak and extensive rebuilding was carried out, extending the pier. The old wharf was removed and the salvaged decking was used to construct a 600-foot shore protection. Ice and ship worm continued to cause considerable damage, as did the many vessels that pulled up to the wharf—passenger steamers and excursion boats, and tugs whose captains liked to tie up overnight, finding a convenient spot from which to seek tows in the morning. A large oil shed was added in 1895. Major repair work was conducted almost every year until the Lighthouse Bureau took over in 1910, when its stringent budget restrictions reduced the number of regular and costly repairs—though the lighthouse was enlarged and refurbished in 1927. The Bureau also conducted the first mainland U.S. experiments with wind-generated electricity at this depot at about the same time. When the Coast Guard took over the Lighthouse Service in 1939, the depot was once again kept in excellent repair.

Following World War II, the U.S. Navy acquired a large interest in the Patuxent area and purchased property around the light station. In 1965, the light was discontinued and the depot was moved to St. Inigoes just inside the Potomac River, where the Coast Guard maintains a small boat station today. Within months the property was turned over to the Navy.

c. 1855, National Archives

The lighthouse dwelling at Point Lookout was built in 1830 by John Donahoo— a small structure along the same lines as the lighthouse at Clay Island. When the station became a depot in 1883 the roof was raised and a second floor was added. Another enlargement of the building to the rear and numerous other improvments to the depot were made in 1927. Major Jared Smith's 1885 photo above shows the small original building. The architectural plans below show the extent of the enlargements made in 1927. The new dwelling would accommodate two families in separate apartments, each with six rooms and an inside bathroom. The then new and popular luxury of hot and cold running water was also added at the same time.

The improvements made to the lighthouse at Point Lookout in 1927 were considered the most extensive restorations ever performed on a Chesapeake Bay lighthouse.

NANSEMOND RIVER 1878-1935 The Nansemond River is located just inside the entrance to the James River. The lighthouse stood off the end of Pig Point at the mouth of the Nansemond. Commercial traffic on the river today is hardly half what it was in the late 1800s when the Board requested funds to construct a hexagonal screwpile lighthouse on the point. The framing of the superstructure of the lighthouse was done at the Lazaretto Depot and loaded aboard the tender *Tulip*, along with the workman needed to assemble the lighthouse. After a 5-day trip down the Bay, the lighthouse arrived at Pig Point and workmen began to erect the house on the metal frame (part of which came from the old lighthouse at Roanoke Marshes, North Carolina).

The design of the cottage-style house was the same as the other screwpile lighthouses on the James River at Deep Water Shoals, White Shoals and Point of Shoals. Engineers determined that the bottom of the river was too hard to use screwpiles, so wooden piles were encased in cast-iron sleeves, as they had been at the York Spit lighthouse. The original lamp was fueled by mineral oil. In1899, a new model 5th-order Fresnel lens was installed to replace the smaller 6th-order lens.

The superstructure was torn down and a steel tower erected on the old foundation in 1935.

c. 1885, Chesapeake Chapter, U.S. Lighthouse Society

BELLS ROCK 1881-1928 Bells Rock lighthouse was located well into the York River channel to assist ships traveling to the town of West Point. The town sits at the end of the York River on the fork of the Pamunkey and Mattaponi Rivers. The dock at West Point was a major terminal for the Richmond and York River Railroad, and an increase of traffic on the York River called for a lighthouse to guide ships to the railroad dock. An appropriation of $35,000 was made to construct the lighthouse in10' of water in the middle of the river just before the fork at West Point. The superstructure for the lighthouse was built at the Lazaretto Depot in November 1880, but was used instead to rebuild the recently burned lighthouse at Thimble Shoal. Another superstructure for Bells Rock was finished at Lazaretto in February of 1881 and towed to theYork River site. The lighthouse was a screwpile hexagonal design with a 4th-order fixed-white light and mechanical fog bell with its assembly housed inside a single dormer. It stood until 1928 when the house was dismantled and replaced by an automated light.The York River is about a mile wide where the lighthouse stood, but after passing West Point, both the Mattaponi and Pamunkey Rivers become narrow ribbons meandering through dense marshes. Today, the upper reaches of the York River around West Point are used almost exclusively by pleasure boats.

Mariners' Museum

National Archives

GREAT SHOALS 1884-1966 The lighthouse at Great Shoals sat at the mouth of Maryland's Wicomico River just off Deal Island's, Dames Quarter Creek (once supposedly called Damned Quarter by Bay pirates). The extensively shoaled area was a narrow sealane for cruise ships and waterman travelling upriver to Salisbury. The lighthouse was a square screwpile structure that was built in a record 32 days. On July 17, 1884, the tender *Jessamine* towed the superstructure from the Lazaretto Depot to the site and the 5th-order lamp was lit on August 15th. The lighthouse was demolished in 1966, after being abandoned for some years.

Mariners' Museum

THE SCREWPILE LIGHTHOUSE DORMER

When looking at screwpile lighthouses, one of the obvious differences in the roofline on each structure is the number of dormer windows. Many had one dormer; others, such as Thomas Point, had as many as four. While the outward appearance looked like a home's dormer windows (with inside area devoted to living space) the lighthouse dormer was more often used to house equipment such as the mechanical fog-bell assembly. Other dormers contained water or fuel tanks, and, in later years, batteries. Many lighthouses had more than one water tank.

The fog-bell assembly room of the Drum Point lighthouse.
Calvert Marine Museum

c. 1882 Mariner's Museum

The Lighthouse Tender HOLLY 1881-1931

No other lighthouse tender served on the Chesapeake Bay as long as the steam sidewheeler *Holly*. The *Holly* was frequently seen in all parts of the Bay and is the tender most often captured in the background of vintage photos of Bay lighthouses, for she supplied the lighthouses and carried inspectors to Bay lighthouses for 50 years—the longest tenure of any lighthouse tender in the United States.

The *Holly* was built at the Canton shipyard of Malster & Reaney, Shipbuilders, Baltimore, in 1881 to replace the supply tender *Heliotrope*, considered too slow to efficiently cruise among the increasing number of lighthouse stations on the Bay. Malster & Reaney had just finished building the *F.C. Latrobe* and the *Annapolis*, steam icebreakers famous as the last sidewheelers used on the Bay. A sistership to the *Holly*, the *Jessamine* was built in the same year at the Malster & Reaney shipyard to serve on the Bay as a construction tender.

Holly was 176' long, with a 24' beam and a draft of 10'. Her hull was built of iron with a wooden superstructure (originally varnished, later painted white). In her 50 years of service she was frequently upgraded—given 3 new boilers, new loading booms and boom engines, rudders, paddlewheels, changes to her interior bulkheads and numerous coats of paint—at the Portsmouth Depot or at a Norfolk or Baltimore shipyard. On the upper deck aft was a large stateroom called The Inspector's Saloon, in obvious deference to the regular use of the *Holly* by the Lighthouse Board Inspector on his rounds to the lighthoues and lightships on the Bay. The Inspector's stateroom, with connecting head and shower, had a double bed and a leather couch. When on board, the Inspector's flag was flown at the head of the boom. The officers bunked in the cabin on the lower deck directly below the Inspector's Saloon. The crew quarters were forward. The usual complement of sailors was 5 officers and 18 crew. The *Holly's* accommodations, particularly the Inspector's Saloon, were apparently comfortable, if not luxurious, since President Grover Cleveland boarded the *Holly* in Annapolis for a number of Bay excursions.

A large mid-ship's storage area on the main deck held the supplies for lighthouses and lightships. On the Bay, most lighthouse keepers could procure their own food on the nearby shore, but Board-mandated equipment and supplies, as well as staples such as oil for lamps, firewood, and coal were brought out to them by the tenders.

Coast Guard

Although she was unsuited for such duty, the *Holly* was used as a lightship at the Bush Bluff station on and off between 1893 and 1895. In February of 1895, while on duty as the lightship, the *Holly* was carried off station by an ice flow and replaced by the converted 2-masted schooner, *Drift*. Almost to the day, 4 years later, another ice flow moved the *Drift* off station, only to be replaced by the *Holly*. When on duty as a lightship, the *Holly's* usual tender duties were performed by the recently launched 164' tender, *Maple*. The only other 5th District supply tender at the time, the older *Violet* was attending to lighthouses in North Carolina. In a twist of roles, the *Maple* attended to both the *Drift* and the *Holly* in 1895 when each was serving as the lightship at Bush Bluff. The use of the unsuitable *Holly* and the converted schooner *Drift* for lightship duty reflected the lack of properly designed lightships on the Bay at the turn of the 19th century.

By 1920, it was apparent to the Lighthouse Board that the *Holly* was no longer equal in performance to the newer steel tenders being built. With her old iron-and-wood hull and slow sidewheel, she was increasingly expensive to maintain and reports began to hint at her replacement. After deciding it was uneconomical to repair her any further, the famous *Holly* was sold on December 4, 1931 for $691. In a small show of recognition, the Lighthouse Board stated in the 1932 annual report that she was sold; "after 50 years of service." The buyer removed most of her deck, including the grand "Inspector's Saloon" and the old reliable hull was renamed *Wright No. 1* and, sadly, used as a barge.

The *Holly* at Point No Point lighthouse in 1910.

The 1900 annual log of the Holly *shows she steamed some 12,602 miles, consuming 905 tons of bituminous coal. She was used 78 days for inspections, 135 days working buoys and attending to lightships, 71 days delivering fuel, rations and supplies to stations, 65 days at lighthouse depots coaling, loading supplies and buoys, and spent 16 days under repair. She worked on 405 buoys, visited 264 light stations, delivered 81 tons of coal to light stations, furnished 10 stations with rations, and inspected 80 stations.*

81

1924, Coast Guard

OLD PLANTATION FLATS 1886-1962

What is called the flats at Old Plantation Shoal is a mile-long sandy shoal running offshore from the entrance to Virginia's Old Plantation Creek and the city of Cape Charles. At the time the lighthouse was built, the shoal ranged in depth from 23' at the south end to 14' at the north end. Engineer (and photographer) Major Jared A. Smith from the Lazaretto Depot recommended that the lighthouse be in 10' of water centered between a bell buoy at the far south end of the shoal and a striped can buoy at the north end. The square screwpile lighthouse was built at a cost of $25,000, a comparatively high price for a screwpile lighthouse at the time. In the winter of 1893, the lighthouse was severely damaged by ice flows, overturning the lantern and the expensive Fresnel lens. The tender *Jessamine* quickly brought another lens. Again in 1918 ice flows damaged the lighthouse, breaking 2 of the 5 piles. Predicting more of the same, the Board reinforced the 5 piles with concrete supports and laid 4,650 tons of stone around the base of the lighthouse at a cost of $37,140— one-and-a-half times the original construction cost.

When compared to the above photo taken in 1924, the 1955 photo to the left, clearly demonstrates how the Coast Guard minimized the cost of maintaining lighthouses by removing the shutters and replacing the original intricate wood bannisters with simple railings. The tender *Holly* is seen steaming away in the top photo.

c.1955, Coast Guard

HOLLAND ISLAND BAR 1889-1960

Holland Island is a fast-eroding island on Maryland's Eastern Shore just across the Bay from Point Lookout. In the late 1800s, the island was a thriving fishing community with 60 homes, a post office, doctor and minister. The island was about 160 acres at the time. Today, it is less than 80 acres with only one home, and it is privately owned by a former waterman and minister, who is hoping to save the island from further erosion. The lighthouse stood off the southern end of the island and acted as a guide into the Kedges Straits. It was a hexagonal cottage-style structure, built at the same time as a similar one for the station at Great Wicomico River, Virginia. Both lights were fabricated at the Lazaretto Depot and delivered to their sites late in the summer of 1889. At the turn of the century the area near the lighthouse was a major oyster dredging and fishing area (it still is, albeit less active) with workboats out of Deal Island and Crisfield using the Kedges Straits into the Bay.

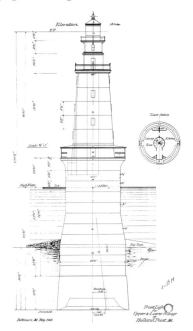

In 1905, the Board looked at the possibility of making the Holland Island station the front light of a range of lights into the Straits. The lighthouse would have been the 51' caisson tower shown in the 1905 design opposite. The Board changed its thinking for it was never built. Instead the Board felt the caisson lighthouse, built at Solomons Lump only 10 years earlier, was sufficient for safe navigation of the straits. The Holland Island screwpile lighthouse remained on station until it was dismantled in 1960, when it was determined that the lighthouse at Solomons Lump alone could serve mariners and Holland Island lighthouse was replaced by an automated light on its old foundation.

Holland Island lighthouse saw more than its share of strange events, beginning with the 1931 murder of the keeper, Ulman Owens, whose naked and dead body was found in his room. A newspaper report of the time stated that the local doctor suggested the keeper may have died of a heart attack, even though a bloody knife lay on the floor and his bruised body indicated that something nefarious transpired at the lighthouse. No stab wound was found, so authorities called the death accidental, but most local folk believed (and still do) that Owens was done in by rum runners. Like some other keepers on the Bay during prohibition, Owens was known to "look the other way" when fast boats sped by his lighthouse at night.

Years later, in the evening of February 19, 1957, 3 U.S. Navy fighter bombers out of the Atlantic City Naval Air Station fired 7 rockets into the lighthouse thinking it was their assigned target "Hannibal," a sunken ship used as a practice target. Fortunately, the rockets did not contain warheads, but the impact of the shells tore three 18" holes in the lighthouse, bent the pilings, and damaged the generator and sleeping quarters. The 4 keepers on duty at the light miraculously managed to escape with scratches and quickly pushed off to the Point Lookout Depot. The lamp continued to burn—at a slight angle.

COBB ISLAND BAR 1889-1940

Cobb Island lies at the mouth of the Wicomico River (Maryland's Western Shore) about half of the way up the Potomac River. The bar stretching up river from the lighthouse was known as one of the best natural oyster beds on the river. Before the lighthouse was built, traffic in this part of the river was heavy with 3 steamboat lines running into the river and numerous ships carrying oysters and tobacco. It was considered a safe harbor from bad weather or drifting ice, but, before the lighthouse was built, ships often hit the edges of the bar at the entrance. The Board concluded that Blackistone Island light, 5 miles downriver, did little to guide ships around the Cobb Island Bar, and the Board requested $15,000 for a lighthouse off the edge of Cobb Island. Construction began on November 1, 1889, and the 4th-order light was lit for the first time on Christmas night. The final cost of the lighthouse (the superstructure was built at Lazaretto) was $25,000. Even with the lighthouse on station, keepers at the lighthouse often reported groundings of sailing ships trying to short-

cut the bar. Maryland State Police reported numerous incidents of oyster-poaching on the popular oyster bar near the light. An entry in the lightkeeper's log noted that "whenever oyster dredging is going on — there's sure to be floating dead bodies seen every week towards the end of the season."

The lighthouse was a square cottage-style structure of the same design as the one built at Tangier Sound, Virginia. In December 1939, the lighthouse burned mysteriously and was so badly damaged that the structure had to be demolished a year later. Rumor had it that the keeper, J. Wilson, dropped a cigarette into the storehouse of cordwood stacked below the lighthouse.

The lighthouse was replaced by a mechanical bell and automatic light. The stone rubble foundation remains and is now appropriately called Lighthouse Lumps.

Coast Guard c. 1900

Perhaps no other river name on the Chesapeake is duplicated as much as "Wicomico." Both Maryland and Virginia have multiple rivers named after the Indian tribe that once inhabited the lower Eastern Shore.

GREAT WICOMICO RIVER 1889-1967

The screwpile lighthouse at Great Wicomico River station sat at the entrance to the small river located on Virginia's Western Shore. It guided mariners through 2 shallow shoals at the entrance to the river. Just inside the river is Cockrell Creek (which takes mariners to Reedville), home of the famous menhaden fishing fleet. The lighthouse was a screwpile cottage-style lighthouse constructed at the Lazaretto Depot at the same time as the Holland Island Bar lighthouse.

Both lighthouses were built on a specially constructed scow, towed to the site of each station, where workers would erect the structures on the screwpile frames. Utilizing what we now call "prefab" building, many screwpile structures were "assembled" on site. A tender would tow the scow (barge) with the lighthouse sections onboard, followed by another scow with a crane, which would lift the pieces of the structure onto the steel screwpile frame. Workers assembled the pre-cut sections and when the basic skeleton was installed, some of the workers could move on to the next job, while others remained to finish the final painting and detail work. The tender would often stand by during construction or return to the site with other parts and equipment. Finally, the tender would bring an engineer who would calibrate and prepare the lamp assembly. The same trip brought the keeper and his family, but the tender stood by until the lamp was fully operable.

The Great Wicomico lighthouse stayed in service until 1967 when it was dismantled and replaced by a flashing light sitting on the original rubble foundation.

Like all lighthouse keepers of the past, Coast Guard keeper J.R. Moore, his engineer and seaman found coffee a necessity of life at the Great Wicomico River lighthouse.

1952 photo by Robert Lunsford

TANGIER SOUND 1890-1961

The lighthouse at Tangier Sound was a square screwpile structure, located off the southern end of Tangier Island, Virginia. The island was first settled by Englishman John Crockett and his family of 4 in 1686. Today the island is home to less than 1,000 persons, almost all of whom make their living from the resources of the Bay.

One of the most unusual collisions with a Bay lighthouse occurred at Tangier Sound when the pungy schooner *Mary L. Colburn* hit the structure in the winter of 1905. The schooner had actually run aground on the bar next to the lighthouse, but when the ice broke, it moved with such force as to virtually catapult the schooner into the lighthouse, entangling the ship's masts with the roof and lantern of the house. The tender *Maple* was called to rescue the keeper and pull the schooner off the house. Days went by with the schooner continuously ramming the structure. Finally the wind direction changed and pulled the schooner away.

The same basic design of Tangier Island lighthouse was later used for the second light at Lower Cedar Point on the Potomac River. The square house structure was a simpler, easier-to-build design than the hexagonal shape, but records are not clear as to why the Board chose one design over another for any one station.

Tangier Island lighthouse stood until 1961, when it was dismantled and replaced by a flashing automatic light standing on the old stone foundation.

c. 1950, Mariner's Museum

SHARKFIN SHOAL 1892-1964 Sharkfin Shoal lies northeast of Bloodsworth Island on Maryland's Eastern Shore in the upper reaches of Tangier Sound. In the late 1800s, it was clear that nearby Clay Island was eroding at a rapid pace and the old lighthouse at the edge of the island would have to be replaced. The Board decided a screwpile lighthouse at the junction of Hooper Strait, Fishing Bay, and the entrances to the Nanticoke and Wicomico Rivers would better serve the numerous waterman in the area. At the same time, a screwpile lighthouse had been designed for Greenbury Point at Annapolis to replace that station's on-land

lighthouse. Both lighthouse superstructures were built at the Lazaretto Depot using the same hexagonal cottage design, though the screwpiles at Sharkfin Shoal were not as difficult to sink and stabilize as those at Greenbury Point. Sharkfin Shoal's 4th-order fixed lamp, 44' off the water, was lit in August of 1892. The house was painted white with a brown roof and green shutters. One of its dormers held a fog bell that was mechanically rung every 15 seconds. The lighthouse served until 1964 when it, too, became a victim of the Coast Guard's replacement program.

Over the years, this remote area of the lower Eastern Shore had 9 lighthouses almost within sight of each other. Their number and proximity are testament to the fishing activity that once dominated these waters. Only the caisson lighthouse at Solomons Lump built in 1895 still stands today.

c. 1962, National Archives

MARYLAND POINT 1892-1954 Fifty miles upriver from the Bay, at a narrow bend of the Potomac River, sat the screwpile lighthouse at Maryland Point. The lighthouse identified an oyster-covered shoal, marked since 1849 with a day marker. Shallow draft ships could sail right over the 10' deep shoal, but larger ships had to go around it, and the danger of faulty calculation called for a

lighthouse. The small hexagonal house was constructed at the Lazaretto Depot and delivered to the site by the tenders *Jessamine* and *Thistle* in the fall of 1892. From past experience, engineers determined the bottom configuration would necessitate the addition of 5'-diameter disks to the screwpiles, with the disks resting on the surface of the shoal. The method was used at other locations where the bottom substrate was hard to penetrate, stablizing the structure while allowing for shorter piles.

The lighthouse was a white house with green shutters and the lantern housed a 4th-order lens. The structure served at the station until 1954 when it was automated. In 1963, it was dismantled carefully by the Coast Guard, piece by piece, and moved to the Portsmouth Depot, although its final home is not known.

During Prohibition, Board reports indicated that some lighthouse keepers on the Potomac River were involved in transporting illegal liquor from Maryland stills across the river to Virginia. Despite revenuers' efforts, rum-running on the river was aggressive. One ferry, the *E.T.Somers* (opposite), was called the "whiskey ferry." When loaded with "St. Mary's Sampler," passengers could hear the clank of bottles in the vehicles, over the din of the ferry's engine.

Lighthouse Tender JESSAMINE 1881-1922 The *Jessamine* was a sistership to the *Holly*, built by the same shipyard in the same year to replace the *Heliotrope* and the *Tulip*, older and slower tenders in the 5th District. Although her design was similar to the *Holly*, the *Jessamine* was intended for service as a construction tender, making repairs, building lighthouses and performing general structural improvements to lighthouses. The *Jessamine* was the primary ship to assist in the construction of new lighthouses and she would normally not have been used for inspections. Her usual crew complement of 4 officers and 12 crew consisted of seamen trained as engineers, carpenters and painters.

The *Jessamine* assisted in building Great Shoals, Cape Charles and Wolf Trap lighthouses on the Bay, and Hog Island lighthouse on the Atlantic coast of Virginia. She also assisted in the building of the keeper's house at Fort Washington and the rebuilding of the wharf at her home port, the Portsmouth Depot. In 1894, she was used to make borings of proposed lighthouses at Point No Point and Smith Point and mapped out the location for the new Solomons Lump lighthouse. In 1900, considered a typical year of service, she installed new lamps at Choptank River, Piney Point, Upper Cedar Point, Bowlers Rock, and Mathias Point and realigned the new lens at Stingray Point. In the same year, she repaired the dock at Washington Wharf and installed a fog signal at Smith Point. Typically, she towed a piledriver or other working boat behind her and spent days anchored next to a building or repair site. She logged 6,217 miles in 1900, half the amount of the *Holly*—a statistic that clearly reveals the two tenders distinct functions.

After 41 years of service, the *Jessamine* was surveyed and condemned as unserviceable. She was sold on March 1, 1922 for $765. Curiously, the *Jessamine's* career ended with some dignity when compared to her famous sistership, the *Holly*. She was first sold to a freight company out of Baltimore and renamed the *Queenstown*. Two years later, the Victor Lynn Line, which operated one of the last freight lines between Baltimore and Salisbury, Maryland, acquired the old *Jessamine* and renamed her, *Victor Lynn*. The lighthouse tender was stripped of her sidewheels and powered with what some say was the first pair of reversible diesel engines on the Bay. She was rebuilt in 1938 and soon thereafter used in the lucrative Caribbean trade, often hauling bananas. At the end of WWII, she returned to the Bay and took up her old route to Salisbury. But the Victor Lynn Company saw that the 15-hour trip from Baltimore to Salisbury was not profitable. Tough competition from motor trucking was threatening all cargo-carrying ships on the Bay. Unlike the *Holly*, the reincarnated lighthouse tender's last trip in 1945 was attended by dignitaries, company officials and newspapermen. She was sold again and last seen in 1957 in Honduras. By then her famed sistership *Holly* was no longer operating.

The *Jessamine* on the railway at the Old Dominion Shipyard, Norfolk, Virginia 1914

PAGES ROCK 1893-1967 Pages Rock light station was located about 5 miles from Yorktown, Virginia, where a shoal juts out from Blundering Point. The increased upriver traffic to West Point—which had resulted in the recent building of the Bells Rock lighthouse—was the rationale for Pages Rock light. Before construction began, engineers determined the bottom was not firm enough to support a lighthouse on screwpiles. Instead, the engineers recommended driving wooden piles to a hard surface below the depth that screws could reach. The superstructure was built at the Lazaretto Depot and delivered to the site by the tenders, *Jessamine* and *Thistle*. The workers built a platform on top of some 80 piles from which construction could be carried out. The pile-driver was placed on the platform and the workers drove the 7 wooden piles and iron sleeves 6' below the surface of the shoal. From the platform, work continued on the superstructure. When most of the construction was finished, the pile-driver was lowered onto its scow by the *Jessamine's* crane. The working platform was removed, purposely leaving a number of the piles standing above the water to act as ice breakers (seen in the photo above). It appears that such platforms were only used in the later years of screwpile construction and only when driving wooden piles for the framing of a foundation.

Pages Rock fell victim to the Coast Guard's automation program and was discontinued in1960. Like many other Bay lights in the early 1960s it was boarded up and stood as a ghostly reminder of better days until 1967, when it was demolished.

Lighthouse Tender MAYFLOWER 1897-1945 The *Mayflower* served mostly in the lower Bay and the Carolina Coast. She was built in1897 to a length of 164 ' and inside her steel hull were twin steam engines, as the days of sidewheelers were over. She was later renamed the *Hydrangea*. The earliest records of ships built as lighthouse tenders date from around 1820. The number of tenders available in the 5th District at any time was 4-7, with most of them assigned to a particular area. Some, such as the *Maple* and the sidewheeler *Violet*, spent much of their career in the Carolinas. The older *Heliotrope*, the *Tulip*, and later, the *Mistletoe*, worked primarily in the southern part of the Bay, while the *Holly* and *Jessamine* were seen all over the Bay. The *Orchid* was used in deep waters and coastal areas. Smaller steam launches, such as the *Bramble,* were used exclusively to supply the gas beacons in Currituck Sound. The *Thistle*, more of a tug actually, was used in shallow waters. Other work boats, such as scows and piledrivers, added to the fleet.

Coninued from page 65

$8,921, was projected to result in a savings of $15,000. Lightship No. 46 spent one last year as a relief vessel on the Bay. Thereafter, the ship disappears from annual lighthouse records. But No. 49 was sent to Massachusetts where it continued to give excellent service at the Hedge Fence station.

In the early part of the nineteenth century, lightships were generally grouped with other floating aids to navigation, including unmanned schooners and buoys. Clearly, as the early nomenclature—"floating lights"—implies, there was a strong inclination to view lightships as only one of several possible kinds of floating aids. As the century wore on, engineers offered some unusual proposals for other floating aids, some of them realized, others not. Some of the designs bespeak the burgeoning of America's cities—for example, the gas buoys that resemble the streetlights one might see on a metropolitan boulevard. In a similar spirit, but on a much more majestic scale, proposals were also made to construct and position huge floating lighthouse towers across the north Atlantic route—an extraordinarily optimistic and grand suggestion, made at a time when the practical applications of structural steel and industrial design seemed limitless. The feasibility of the lighted trans-Atlantic boulevard was apparently studied, and in 1876, at the Centennial Exhibition in Philadelphia, the public's imagination was teased with drawings and vivid paintings of enormous lighted towers, dramatically lighting a tempestuous ocean. The towers were to be manned and operated as communication centers and research stations, as resting places for great ocean-going vessels— even, as anchors during storms. The mammoth floating lighthouse had its brief mo-

Continued on page 95

c. 1948, Collection P. Hornberger

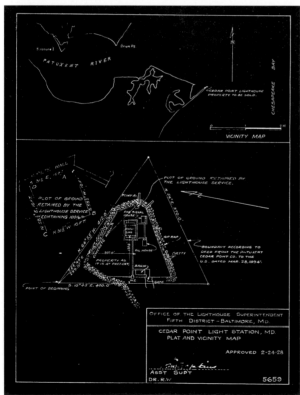

CEDAR POINT 1896-1928

Surely one of the most beloved lighthouses of the Chesapeake Bay, the Cedar Point lighthouse was commissioned in 1896—late in the Chesapeake Bay's lighthouse history—and the cottage and rooftop lantern were one of a kind among the Bay's many lighthouses. Built on stone foundation piers, the brick first and second-stories supported a wood-framed, shingled third level and a steeply pitched and gabled, slate-tiled roof. A square frame tower rose from one corner of the roof, holding a 4th-order Fresnel light, a guide for congested traffic in and out of the Patuxent at the turn of the century.

Cedar Point light is one of the shorter-lived lighthouses of the Chesapeake region, and this largely because of changes in the shoreline, including the natural erosion of the point. In 1928 the lighthouse station was replaced by an automated post beacon. The empty lighthouse deteriorated slowly, gradually engulfed by the Bay. In the 1950s, the post beacon was removed because of sand dredging nearby and a light was placed in the old fog-bell tower. When, in 1957, the bell tower collapsed in a storm, the light was replaced by a bell buoy. At this time the lighthouse property fell under jurisdiction of the expanding Patuxent Naval Air Station.

For years, local lighthouse lovers stood sadly and helplessly by as the lighthouse, entirely surrounded by water, succumbed to the ravages of wind, weather and wave. Year after year, boat excursions were made to the lighthouse, carrying folks eager for one last look. In 1981, the lantern was removed by the

Continued next page

Calvert Marine Museum

The above 1904 photograph is the earliest known image of Cedar Point and one of the few of the station in active service. It shows the dangerously close shoreline, the large separate fog-signal tower in front and the oil house and privy in back. The 1980 photo (below) shows the Calvert Marine Museum's buyboat, *Wm. B. Tennyson*, going by the lighthouse surrounded by water.

Navy and, in 1984, was dedicated to the Naval Air Test Museum.

In 1996, when the remaining lighthouse structure was about to be demolished, the Navy responded to requests to bequeath the sunburst decorations on the gabled ends of the upper structure of the lighthouse and other surviving architectural details to the Calvert Marine Museum. On October 17, 1996, a crane lifted the upper floor and roof of the lighthouse off the crumbling substructure and it was barged to the Calvert Marine Museum. Relatively few bricks were saved—a corner of the lighthouse and part of the chimney. The Calvert Marine Museum, which now also owns the Cove Point lighthouse station, will eventually use the lighthouse remnants in a permanent exhibit. Some of the old brick—made for the lighthouse in the 1890s by the Calvert Brick Company of Solomon's—is to be used in a new pavilion.

In 1997, loss of the ruined lighthouse—which had been a day marker for mariners—prompted Chesapeake Bay watermen to complain of the danger that the remnant foundation piers, riprap, and toppled bricks posed. As of this writing, the area remains unlighted, marked only as hazardous on navigational charts.

Calvert Marine Museum

ANNAPOLIS DEPOT 1896-1937 The lighthouse depot at Annapolis was established to store and maintain buoys between Sandy Point and the Patuxent River. It was located on a point of land on the east side of the Severn River and Little Kerr's Creek (now Carr's Creek), just inside Greenbury Point. The Greenbury Point lighthouse was just downriver. The depot was on land leased to the government by Circuit Court Judge James Hunter and originally used by the Naval Academy as an experimental battery. Immediately next to the land was Fort Madison, one of a number of small fortifications built around the mouth of the Severn River to protect the port of Annapolis and the Naval Academy. In the spring of 1896, the superintendent of the Naval Academy was ordered to turn the land over to the lighthouse establishment with the condition that the land be used only for Lighthouse Board purposes. A further condition stated that the War Department could take back the property if needed for defense. It is not known why the Navy was suspicious about the possibility of the land being used for anything other than lighthouse activities, but, perhaps, their possessiveness reflected turf battles between the two growing services.

The depot contained a custodian's dwelling, a buoy shed, a workshop, a henhouse and privy. The property was completely surrounded by a wire and board fence. The wharf stretched 450' out into the Severn River with a tramway built to move buoys and supplies directly on cars to and from the buoy shed. Spar buoys from the Portsmouth Depot were stored here to temporarily replace the can and nun buoys during severe winters. Tall wooden spar buoys could withstand the pressures of ice, but metal buoys at that time were subject to being crushed and swallowed by the Bay.

The Annapolis depot operated until the late 1930s when the Navy Department pressured the government to return the property for use as a naval station and proving ground. Only a few years earlier the lighthouse at Greenbury Point was decommissioned. The Naval Academy retains the property to this day.

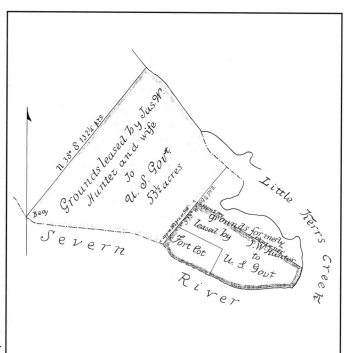

94

WASHINGTON WHARF, 1907-1945 The Washington, D.C. lighthouse depot was referred to as Washington Wharf, indicating a less-than-depot status among lighthouse facilities on the Bay. The wharf was owned by the federal government before its transfer to the Lighthouse Board, who wanted it as a storage facility for the smaller buoys and equipment needed for the upper Potomac River. It also served as overnight dockage for tenders. The wharf was located on Water Street at the foot of O Street. No custodian lived on the property. The building was a 65' x 33' frame structure covered with corrugated galvanized iron. The journey up the Potomac from the Bay to Washington D.C. took more than a full day, so it is easy to see why the Board felt a need for a storage and docking facility at Washington. As tenders became more efficient, it was easier for them to work and supply the upper river and the wharf was discontinued during WWII.

---

ment in engineering consciousness, but, in the end, lightships remained ships and electronic signals solved problems of position and communication—in other words, the problems of isolation (though it might be said that the romance of these lonely communication centers has come to fruition in our twentieth century space stations).

It is interesting to recall that the Lighthouse Board presided at a time when a close link between theoretical and applied science obtained, and was, perhaps, more easily apprehended by the lay person. Tinkering with new designs, exploring and testing—both ideas and innovative equipment—seems to have been endemic to the lighthouse service. The general depot at Staten Island was often used for research and development work, but other depots were important, including Lazaretto at Baltimore and Portsmouth in Hampton Roads. Every apparatus in use by the lighthouse service was studied and, if possible, improved. Of special note during the 1870s was the growing use of the steam whistle . The Board was truly surprised at the strength of sound produced by the whistling buoy. "The effect due to the percussion of the water in driving out the air is much greater than was thought possible before an examination of the apparatus in actual operation. The size of the whistle...also gives a volume of sound which can be heard at the distance of several miles, even against an ordinary wind."[16]

The tools of experimental research were not so specialized—in fact, they generally included at least some component of careful, natural observation, accessible to all. Thus, some of the practical research that the lighthouse establishment sponsored was, as they liked to report, of genuine importance to the advance of theory. Certainly, it made for interesting

Continued on page 101

95

RAGGED POINT 1910-1962 Ragged Point lighthouse, the last screwpile lighthouse built on the Chesapeake Bay, was located just off Ragged Point on the Potomac River across the river from Piney Point Lighthouse station. As early as 1835, the Board was in dispute about placing a lightship at Ragged Point vs. building a lighthouse at Piney Point. The Piney Point lighthouse was built, but years of mariner's requests for a light at Ragged Point were to no avail, as Congress argued that mariners could adequately navigate the area by drawing a line between the Piney Point and Blackistone Island lights. Finally, in 1896, after ceaseless complaints, and a few accidents, the Board requested $20,000 to build a lighthouse and fog signal at the point. Instead, an appropriation of $15,000 was approved in 1906. Another $15,000 was approved in 1907, and an additional $5,000 in 1908. In the end, after years of congressional delay, the lighthouse cost $34,224, almost $15,000 more than the original estimate. Finally, in 1910, the 4th-order light was lit in the new screwpile lighthouse.

Early evidence of the Board's disappointment in the longevity of screwpile lighthouses is shown in the caisson structure (opposite) proposed in 1896, the same year that the Board first requested funds for a light at Ragged Point. Like the proposed caisson for the Choptank River lighthouse, a cottage-style house would have been placed on a traditional caisson base. In fact, no such combination was ever built on the Bay.

Ironically, Ragged Point, the final screwpile lighthouse placed on the Bay, was one of the first to be decommissioned under the Coast Guard automation program in 1962.

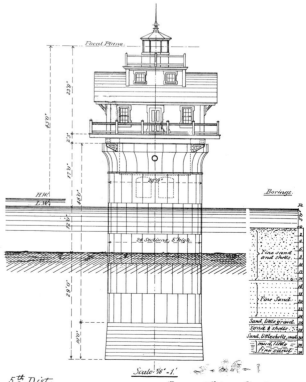

The *Manzanita* class of lighthouse tenders had finer lines and more powerful engines than their predecessors, resulting in faster speeds and better maneuverability.

Coast Guard

Lighthouse Tender ORCHID Built in 1908, by the New York Shipbuilding Company at a cost of $192,000, the *Orchid* was one of seven sisterships built that year known as the *Manzanita* class of steel tenders. At 190' with a 13' draft, the *Orchid* was the largest lighthouse tender to serve on the lower Bay and the Atlantic Ocean. She had a maximum speed of 12 knots from twin coal-burning steam engines generating 1,000 HP. Her crew complement consisted of 39 seaman and 3 officers. This class of tender was designed with vertical sides to provide a flat surface for ease in lifting buoys—reducing the tendency of buoys to slide beneath the ship. The forecastle deck had rounded edges to prevent the buoy cage from catching in the process of hauling. Extra large steel booms replaced the wooden booms used on previous tenders, and wire rope replaced manilla to haul the newer, heavier buoys. The *Orchid* was stationed at the Portsmouth Depot and used on and off the Bay most of her career until 1945, when she was transferred to the Philippines.

In 1930, the *Orchid* steamed almost 12,000 miles and, in the same year, her boilers were replaced at a cost of $40,000. The photo above shows the *Orchid* around 1920 under the Lighthouse Service (note the service's insignia on the bow), with her original black hull and white superstructure, while the photo to the right shows her in the 1940s' wartime-gray paint scheme.

In the spring of 1922, one of the Orchid's seamen, James F. Kelly, jumped overboard and rescued a 9-year-old newspaper boy, who had fallen overboard at the Portsmouth Depot. Kelly's action was recognized in the Annual Report to the Secretary of Commerce.

Mariners' Musuem

97

National Archives

CAPE CHARLES & CHESAPEAKE LIGHTSHIP STATIONS 1888-1965

The original Cape Charles lightship station was locally called Smith Island Shoal (not for Smith Island, Maryland, but Smith Island, Virginia). It was located 9 miles from Cape Charles lighthouse, off Virginia's lower Eastern Shore, marking the north side of the entrance to the Bay. In 1928, the station was moved to accommodate deeper-draft ships, improving the sea lanes on approach to the Bay. The final station position was near Cape Henry lighthouse and renamed Chesapeake. Together the two stations served mariners for 77 years, representing the longest maintained lightship station on the Bay, and, ultimately, the last on the Bay.

LIGHTSHIP No. 80 was first stationed at Cape Lookout Shoals (just south of Cape Hatteras) from 1905 until 1924. For the next 3 years she served at Cape Charles. Built in New York in 1904, and delivered to the Lazaretto Depot, insufficient operating funds kept her at the depot until the following year. In 1927, she was replaced at Cape Charles by No. 72 lightship, which had been on relief duty. No.80 is also shown above in a later configuration (with the bow-piece removed) during the time she served at the Cape Charles station.

98

National Archives

Mariners' Museum, Ralph Smith Collection

The ubiquitous Lightship No.46 was the first ship to serve the Cape Charles station. It was followed by Lightships No.49, No.101, and, later, when the station was moved and renamed Chesapeake, by Lightships No.80, No.72, and, finally, Lightship No.116. During WWI the U.S. Navy minesweepers, *Owl* and *Brant*, served at the station, and, though outfitted with lights, their wartime purpose was the examination of ships entering the Bay.

Lightship No.80 (opposite page), a 129' lightship built in 1904, served at Cape Charles from 1924 to1927 after a thorough overhaul at Portsmouth Depot. Both of her old lamp-houses were removed and replaced with deckhouses, her masts were refitted with new electric lamps and the flared bow-piece was removed, exposing the original bow configuration. The bow piece was installed to soften the effect of waves and throw spray away from the ship.

After moving the station location, renaming it, and painting *Chesapeake* on her hull, Lightship No.116 (above and next page) took over and served for 29 years, (except for 3 years during WWII when a lighted buoy was in place). She was a 133' ship, built in1930 by the Charleston Drydock & Machine Company in South Carolina for a contract price of $274,434. No.116 was powered by a diesel electric engine driven by four 75-kilowatt diesel generators. She swung a 5'9" propeller, pushing the ship at speeds up to 10 knots—a far improved speed over the old schooner-rigged lightships of the past. She stayed on the Chesapeake station until 1965 when she was replaced by the "Texas tower" lighthouse still standing at the mouth of the Chesapeake Bay. No.116 went on to close another lightship station at the mouth of the Delaware Bay in 1970, after which she was decommissioned.

After 40 years of service, No.116 was transferred to the National Park Service and put on display at Haines Point, Washington, D.C. In 1982 she was moved to Baltimore's Inner Harbor as part of the Baltimore Maritime Museum. No.116 is listed as a National Historic Landmark.

LIGHTSHIPS ASSIGNED TO CAPE CHARLES OR CHESAPEAKE STATIONS:

1888-1891 #46
1891-1916 #49
1916-1924 #101
1924-1927 #80
1927-1933 #72
1933-1942 #116
1942-1945 buoy
1945-1965 #116

Highlights of events at the Cape Charles/ Chesapeake lightship station:

• *1896 — No.49's anchor parted– she drifted 16 miles south of Cape Henry.*

• *1898 — No.49 was blown off station and picked up off Currituck, North Carolina.*

• *1912 — No.49 was rammed by SS Grayson.*

• *1927 — No.80's deckhouse, radio room damaged during severe winter storm—seas flooded engine room and demolished all auxiliary boats.*

• *1936 — No.116 was blown off station during a hurricane, dropped spare anchor and steamed ahead for 10 hours to reduce dragging.*

Collection P. Hornberger

CHESAPEAKE LIGHTSHIP No.116 may be seen in the water at the Baltimore Maritime Museum in Baltimore's Harbor Place. She is on display along with the U.S. Coast Guard Cutter *Roger Brook Taney* and the U.S.S. Submarine *Torsk*.

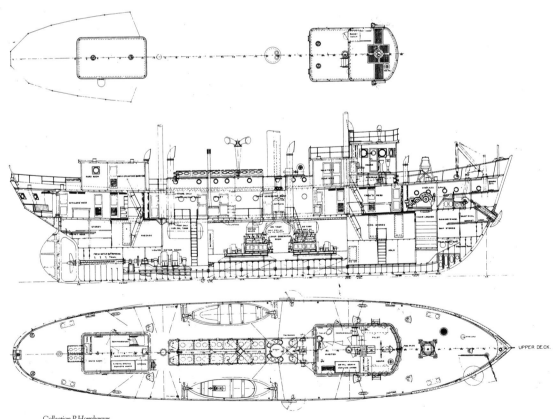

 Collection P. Hornberger

National Archives

Every fog-horn apparatus, including those on lightships, was tested for its effectiveness.

Continued from Page 96

reading at the end of their annual reports. Of special note and affection was the work of Joseph Henry, distinguished member of the original Lighthouse Board (later its president) and secretary of the Smithsonian Institution, whose reports "relative to fog signals" appeared in appendices to the annual reports in 1874 and 1877 and were the subject of much debate—and even spirited disagreement with a fellow investigator at Britain's celebrated Trinity House.

Sometimes, the Lighthouse Board had the opportunity to encourage cooperation and collaboration on scientific investigations with other government agencies, even, on one occasion, involving the keepers in a collaborative effort to collect data for the U.S. Geological Survey regarding an August, 1886 earthquake that badly damaged two New Jersey lights. They sent a questionnaire to all "light-keepers throughout the region affected," and condensed and printed them as an appendix to the 1886 report. The Chesapeake Bay keepers offered an intriguing array of observations made at the time of the quake—a feather duster that began to swing, a clock that was stopped by the shocks, a shaking wharf, rattling windows, and very precise

estimates of the time of occurrence—all in all, quite remarkable testimony to a high degree of watchfulness and alertness.[17]

In 1890, preparations for the World's Columbian Exposition of 1893 were well underway when the Lighthouse Board received a letter from the chairman of the World's Fair Committee asking "what exhibit the Lighthouse Board could make at the World's Fair," and how much this would cost.[18] The Lighthouse Board, then at the very pinnacle of self-assuredness, promptly responded that "to make a proper exhibit...it would need an allotment of 5,000 square feet of wall and floor space and $15,000 in money"—a request that the organizers apparently thought excessive.[19] How, the organizers wanted to know, was the exhibit going to differ from the 1876 Centennial Exposition in Philadelphia?

Members of the Board were clearly offended. "No part of the shores of this land is without...evidence of the Board's care," they complained in their annual report, "no channel exists which does not contain its buoys, and turn where we may by sea, there we find the forethought of the Board and its efforts

Continued on page 105

101

c. 1913, Coast Guard

The iron mesh hoops at the mastheads of early lightships were day markers. On the Bay the hoops were usually painted black to contrast with the sky.

BUSH BLUFF 1891-1918 Bush's Bluff or Bushe's Bluff station was located in the lower Bay, in the Elizabeth River just over a mile north of Craney Island, and served as a mark to the approaches to both Norfolk and Portsmouth harbors. The first ship assigned to the station was Lightship No.46, although the tender *Holly* temporarily served soon after. But the converted Coast & Geodetic 80' schooner, *Drift* (later numbered No. 97), shown above, soon took over after it was clear the *Holly* was unsuited for such duty. From 1893-1895 all three ships served alternately at Bush Bluff. Both the *Drift* and No.46 were used extensively at other Bay stations. Bush Bluff station was discontinued in1918, with the *Drift* condemned and laid up. Lightship No.46 went on to serve at Tail of the Horseshoe station and to further relief duty. The lightship station was replaced with a lighted buoy in1918.

c. 1915, National Archives

Lightship No.46
served at 5
stations
on the Bay:

1888-1891 Cape Charles
1891-1893 Bush Bluff
1893-1895 Wolf Trap
1895-1897 Smith Point
1901-1922 Tail
  of Horseshoe

TAIL OF THE HORSESHOE 1900-1922 The Tail of the Horseshoe is an extensive shoal lying between the Thimble Shoal and the northbound Chesapeake channels, just inside the entrance to the Bay. Two lightships served the station for 22 years: No.71 and No.46. The 122' No.71 was built in 1897 and served at Tail of the Horseshoe for only one year, beginning in 1900. In 1918, while serving at Diamond Shoal in North Carolina, the German submarine U-104 gave No.71's crew ample time to abandon ship in its lifeboats before sinking it.

   No.46 (shown above and below) served the station from 1901-1922. She was built in 1887 along with a sistership, No.45. She served at 5 different stations on the Bay (see opposite page, Bush Bluff) and ended as a relief ship when the Tail of the Horseshoe station was discontinued in 1922. In 1923, she was sold in Norfolk for use as a cargo ship, rigged with topmasts and bowsprits and renamed the *W.T.Bell*. In 1927, the *Bell* was bound from Halifax, N.S. to New York when she ran aground. Her cargo consisted of 25 large wooden kegs of blended whiskey.

c. 1915 National Archives

c. 1916 National Archives

35 FOOT CHANNEL 1908-1919 The only lightship to serve at the 35 Foot Channel station was ship No.45. The station was established as a junction mark for ships westbound for the York River entrance and northbound via the busy main Chesapeake channel, after entering the Bay. She was a 124' steel-frame, oak-planked schooner-rigged ship built at Linwood, Pennsylvania in 1887. Her sistership was No.46. No.45 was originally assigned to Winter Quarter Shoal, off Assateague Island. In1908, having been surveyed and considered unsuitable for offshore duty, she was reassigned to the new station at 35 Foot Channel. After 11 years on station, she went into the Portsmouth Depot for repairs. There, another ship at the depot caught fire and drifted against her, causing considerable damage. She was then considered uneconomical to repair, condemned and sold for scrap. The station was discontinued in1919, replaced by a lighted whistle buoy.

Coast Guard

In a heavy fog, early lightship crews had to hand-operate the fog-bell for incessant hours

to protect and care, not only for the trade of its own country, but also for the commerce of the world." In fact, the report states testily, the Board "preferred to make no exhibit if it could not make one worthy of the Light-House Establishment and this last Worlds Fair.[20] But, in the end, the Lighthouse Board made do with a space 24 by 51 feet (only a little over 1,200 square feet), though they confess, without the slightest embarrassment, that "the aisles were encroached upon by moving the railing on one side 3 feet 6 inches and on the other side 1 foot 9 inches."[21]

In many ways, the Board was correct in calling attention to "vast improvements" in the navigational aids, which guided mariners on the seacoasts, bays, Great Lakes, and rivers of the United States—and the century's end offered an irresistible moment to present a summing-up. "Improvements of great importance have been made in illuminating apparatus, in buoys, in tenders and light-ships, etc.," the Board noted. "For example, since 1876, lard oil has almost entirely disappeared

and been replaced by mineral oil, and therefore the lamps have all had to be changed; bell, whistling, and gas buoys, unknown at that time, have come into common use; lightships are beginning to have their own steam motive power, and a start has been made in the application of electricity as an illuminating agent for them; and of lenses instead of reflectors for their light."[22]

Even so, it is perhaps significant that the Lighthouse Board chose to look backward over its long history at the Columbia Exposition, rather than forward, into the next century—and perhaps an unpropitious sign, as well, regarding their future prospects, for the Columbia Exposition did not celebrate the end of a glorious innovative age so much as herald a giant leap into the accelerated tempos and unprecedented technological changes of the twentieth century. But the Board made no bones about its part in "this last World's Fair:" in terms of aids to navigation, they had built and sustained the best of all possible worlds. There was no room for

Continued on page 108

105

RELIEF SHIPS were available in each district to relieve the assigned ship when it was temporarily absent from its station. In the early years, due to the time required to repair wooden ships, the relief period was often for months. In some cases, relief vessels actually served longer at the station than the assigned ship. Relief ships were designed no differently than other lightships and a large number of ships continually changed status, and name, from relief ship to assigned-station ship. Both relief ships on this page were also renamed and assigned to the Cape Charles station during their careers.

RELIEF SHIP No.72 (top of page and interior views opposite) was a 123' steam-powered, steel-hull lightship built in 1900 in Massachusetts. She was originally stationed at Diamond Shoal, North Carolina, and later served as temporary light at Overfalls, Delaware and at Cape Lookout Shoals, North Carolina. She served as a relief ship in the 5th District from 1922-1927 and was assigned to both Cape Charles and the Chesapeake stations between 1927-1933. She was transferred to Cross Rip, Massachusetts, in 1934 and retired from duty in 1937. An indication of the versatility of relief ships was evident in her 1907 passage to the Staten Island Depot to pick up supplies for all the lighthouses in the 5th District, a duty normally reserved for the lighthouse tenders.

RELIEF SHIP No.49 (opposite), which served on Cape Charles station from 1891-1916, also served as a relief ship in the 5th District from 1916-1925. She was built in 1891 (originally for service at Bush Bluff), of composite wood and steel, with a schooner rig showing 2 oil lamps. She is shown here at the Portsmouth Depot in 1917, after being converted to acetylene lamps. She went on to serve in Massachusetts waters where she was rammed and sunk just after she arrived. Later raised and returned to service, she was retired in 1941 after serving for 50 years.

In 1898, while serving at the Cape Charles lightship station, No.49's annual log reported that she was passed by 3,268 steamers, 10 ships, 45 barks, 8 brigs, and 7,950 schooners.

Ward Room – a room used by the officers for relaxation or dining

Radio Shack – the room where all radio equipment is operated. The operator, was often refered to as "sparky."

Crew's Mess – a room or space for crew dining. Old English naval lore says the label comes from the condition of the eating area when a meal is served in a rough sea.

The officer's ward room on Lightship No.72 was almost luxurious for its time. The loose bow-back chairs must have been stowed in a storm, as in August of 1924, when No.72 was serving on relief at the mouth of the Bay. The captain reported that she was dragged off station in hurricane-force winds and was completely submerged several times. In1927, while on the Cape Charles station, a severe winter storm broke open the ports in the after-house, flooding the radio shack and engine room. The lower-deck level, looking forward to the anchor windlass, held the crew's mess. Notice the fences (called "fiddles") on the crew's tabletop to hold items while at sea.

RELIEF LIGHTSHIP No.2 The lightship shown above at Norfolk is No.2 relief ship, originally the 98' schooner *General Taylor* that was probably built in the mid-1800s. She was converted to a lightship and first assigned to the station at Pollock Rip, Massachusetts. She later served a year at Winter Quarter Shoal and returned to Massachusetts. Transferred to Delaware in 1907, she came to the 5th District in1910, serving the next 11 years out of the Portsmouth Depot. Other than being struck by the tug, *Emma Kate Ross*, in 1915 while serving at Bush Bluff, little is known about her activity on the Bay. She represents one of a number of relief vessels moving in and out of the Bay. Records indicate lightships (unassigned to stations) carrying the numbers12, 16, 21, 23, 28, 52, and 91 served at least some time on the Bay—or spent time at either Lazaretto or Portsmouth Depots awaiting orders.

improvement—and they said as much.

For the Chesapeake Bay in particular, there is some truth to their observations. Few lighthouses were built on the Chesapeake following the turn of the century. The Baltimore Light caisson, which had fallen on its side at the bottom of the Bay and was abandoned by all save the insurers of the original contractor, was finally righted and put into commission in 1908. Now there remained only the 1914 completion of the Thimble Shoal caisson (though not a new light station) to bring an end to all lighthouse construction on the Bay—that is, with one notable exception, the Texas-tower light station that likewise replaced the Chesapeake lightship in 1964. Thus, although it can be said that the Board was truly responsible for lighting the Bay, much of their work, ironically, did not

survive the technological innovations that were, even then, close at hand. The small and docile screwpile cottage—the practical solution that the Board found for so much of the Bay's robust regional commerce and ship traffic, for its numerous and convenient waterways, as well as its extensive and inconvenient shoals—was the very idealization of a bustling mid-19th century, semi-rural or small-town way of life.

Following the World's Fair in Chicago, the Board's cumbersomeness was becoming all too apparent to others, and by 1903, the unwieldy and increasingly contentious administrative establishment had been moved to the Department of Commerce, where plans were in the offing to revamp the entire lighthouse service[23] In this final work, the Board contributed its own peculiar brand of *noblesse oblige*:

The Portsmouth Depot was home port to the tenders and lightships of the 5th District. For the first 15 years of the depot's operations, it leased limited docking space from a private owner, until, finally, in 1885, its own dock was built with 21,960 ' of decking. Tenders and relief ships were able to quickly move north into the Chesapeake Bay, south to the Carolinas, or into the Atlantic Ocean from this central location. The original depot property was traded later with the City of Portsmouth for the current location of the Coast Guard's 5th District headquarters a few blocks away. The Coast Guard no longer refers to such aids-to-navigation facilities as "depots," preferring instead to use the all-encompassing label, "support center."

ponderous deliberations and exhaustively reasoned recommendations. In 1910, the Lighthouse Bureau was formally composed and a new administrative era began under the able leadership of George R. Putnam. Looking back from some distance at the long years of the Lighthouse Board, Putnam attempted a summing up of the problems the Board had engendered—too many officers, too many reports, too much detail, too much pontificating: "The workings of a bureaucratic mind," he wrote, "when given a free hand, sometimes lead to wide departures from simplicity."[24]

The 1907 inventory of the Fifth District counted:

• 226 lighthouses and beacon lights, including 35 post lanterns

• 5 light vessels in position

• 2 light vessels for relief

• 15 day beacons

• 1,290 other buoys in position

• 3 tenders for supply and inspection

• 2 tenders for construction and repair

• 1 steamer to supply gas to beacons in the North Carolina Sound

• 1 sharpie to supply beacons

By the time of the Philadelphia sesquicentennial celebration, in 1926, the automation of lighthouses on the Chesapeake Bay had begun and lighthouse construction had virtually come to an end. The first Fresnel lens used in America was on display in the Lighthouse Service's booth, along with the first fog signal used in 1719. Interestingly, the large bell buoy dwarfs the lighthouse model and the first-order lens, a true reflection of things to come.

CHAPTER IV

By the time of the reorganization of the Lighthouse Service in 1910, a one-hundred year period of lighthouse construction on the Chesapeake Bay had essentially drawn to a close. At this time, the lighthouses and lighthouse keepers surely seemed an immutable part of the Bay's landscape, and yet, in that odd way of American development and progress, just as the work of lighting the Bay seemed to have reached a fair degree of completion, an approximately fifty-year period of dismantling the work of the preceding half century was about to begin. For this reason, it is perhaps one of the most interesting periods in lighthouse history, one which has many parallels in other occupations that have slowly and silently vanished, eliminated by technology that renders the human performance of work obsolete. Inevitably, the lighthouse most likely to vanish was the screwpile cottage, the signature light of the Chesapeake Bay, and a fact that irrevocably altered its maritime landscape.

The new Commissioner of Lighthouses, George R. Putnam, brought a fresh management style to the administration of the lighthouse establishment: forward-looking and unpretentious, thorough but smoothly efficient. He brought a new vocabulary, too, especially to personnel relations, and the key word—the one that replaced the Board's central organizing principle of *discipline*—was *morale*. At the top of his list, in every annual report, were his written estimations of what needed to be done to ensure that lighthouse service personnel maintained a high degree of commitment, loyalty and satisfaction in their work, and he lobbied successfully for higher wages, retirement and medical benefits (through the U.S. Public Health Service) as well as for much-needed disability compensation. Each

year the U.S. Employees' Compensation Commission published figures that, indeed, showed substantial loss of life and injuries resulting in permanent disability to lighthouse field personnel (certainly far beyond any other civil service occupation), statistics that Putnam unfailingly included in each report as indicative of the hazardous nature of lighthouse work. In Putnam's enlightened view, the energy and productivity of his employees depended on good working conditions and fair compensation. Thus, the tables were turned: where the Lighthouse Board had emphasized duty and respect toward the government, Putnam's focus was on the obligation of the government as employer to the lighthouse personnel.

Not surprisingly, Putnam's successful negotiations won for him the admiration and unswerving loyalty of his employees. But there was an interesting trade-off in his efforts to secure the necessary appropriations, and one whose end he perhaps did not entirely foresee: to wit, a very strong push for economy—so strong, in fact, that he has sometimes been compared to the tightwad Pleasonton. Putnam's administrative skill makes this comparison unfair. His tenure spanned the First World War when appropriations were trimmed and, later, the Depression, when economy was a way of life. What is true, however, is that the repair and maintenance of lighthouse property suffered from strict budgetary policies. Throughout the 1920s, inflation and labor unrest were pandemic, encouraging attention to employees' demands as well as to the economic benefits of automation.

In 1922, Putnam complained vigorously that the salaries of Lighthouse Service employees "did not offer sufficient compensa-

The signature lighthouse of the Bay, the screwpile cottage, would soon vanish.

CHESAPEAKE & DELAWARE CANAL LIGHTS 1892-1927 Until the end of the19th century, ships had to enter and leave the Bay by making the long passage to and from the mouth of the Bay. In1892, the privately held Chesapeake & Delaware Canal Company finished digging the14 miles from the end of the Elk River to Delaware Bay. The technology of the times was limited to the use of locks, and ships were towed by mule on a parallel path. One such lock, located at Chesapeake City, was known as the Maryland Lock (shown above). At either end of the lock was a 33' wooden light-tower containing a kerosene lamp raised by a block-and-tackle system from inside the structure. The keeper of the light was the lock tender, living on the premises, and paid by the company from proceeds of canal tolls. In 1919, the U.S. government took over control of the canal when the private owners could not finance the massive cost of converting the outdated lock system to a sea-level canal. After years of widening, dredging and building bridges over the canal, the new sea-level canal opened in 1927 and its navigational aids came under control of the Lighthouse Service. Without the locks, the canal tenders and light keepers were no longer needed. In1940, one year after the transfer of the Lighthouse Service, the Coast Guard began a program of widening the canal and improving the navigational lights. Today, the canal is a busy northern entrance to the Chesapeake Bay with pilots out of Chesapeake City guiding over1,000 ships through the canal annually. A full size replica of the canal's "light towers," along with a history of the canal, can be seen at the C&D Canal Museum in Chesapeake City.

tion to attract to it a personnel suited to its special needs, nor to retain many who do enter it."[1] Of particular irritation were the pay increases received by the military services, especially the Navy, to whom the Lighthouse Service was subject to transfer in times of war. "At present," Putnam complained, "officers in the Lighthouse Service ... are in some cases receiving less than half the compensation of persons in other services in similar status and with no greater responsibilities or requirements."[2]

Against the background of Prohibition, now a reality, Putnam took care to note that he was asking for disability benefits only "to cover cases, not due to vicious habits or misconduct..."[3] It is, in fact, a safe bet that quite

a bit of bootleg whiskey and other spiritous liquors made their way along the tributaries of the Bay and across the Bay itself, and quite possible that more than one lighthouse keeper was culturally disposed, if not economically enticed, to look the other way as the forbidden libations were transported to the urban speakeasies and rural inns that everywhere responded to what seemed an insatiable demand.

A veritable champion of the Civil Service, Putnam emphasized fairness and equity in all matters relating to personnel, and, in his own Bureau, he was careful to include both field and clerical employees in requests for improved benefits. "There is," he pointed out, "provision for retirement of persons incapacitated for duty in the Coast Guard and in the Army and Navy."[4] Additionally, Putnam stressed the need for "medical relief" for those lightkeepers at stations too remote to allow them to reach the hospitals and stations of the Public Health Service. Finally, Putnam wished to see "adjustment, within a moderate amount, of claims by lighthouse employees for loss or damage to personal property... caused by storms, collisions, or fire at light stations, depots, and on vessels" as well as "certain necessary privileges...accorded by law to similar services, including the purchase of commissary supplies, transportation of families and of household effects when ordered to change station permanently, and transportation on Army transports."[5]

Nevertheless, the drive for cost-efficiency had made personnel cutbacks particularly attractive. For seven years, the lighthouse service was maintained on annual appropriations less than those for 1911, when, according to Putnam, savings "were effected by the discontinuance of 11 local offices and 5 tenders of the service, and a reduction of 200 in the number of employees..."[6]

In 1922, Putnam noted a six percent reduction in the number of lightkeepers (from 1,530 to 1,443). Thereafter, the replacement of keepers with automated equipment began to be a regular feature of Putnam's annual report on "economies in operation." The number of automatic lights and buoys increased steadily. "These," he said, "are operated at greatly reduced cost of maintenance and without loss of efficiency as compared with lights attended by keepers."[7] At the same time, Putnam's efforts to improve the salaries and benefits of his employees allowed him to point to "important improvement in the efficiency and morale of the personnel of the Lighthouse Service." In 1925, disability retirement was granted.[8]

Between 1910 and 1922, ninety-five lighthouse stations had been "changed from attended to automatic." The loss of keepers on the Chesapeake Bay between 1922 and 1932 is notable, dropping seventeen percent, while stations with keepers dropped by twenty-two percent.[9] Thus, although the U.S. Coast

Coast Guard

To commemorate the 100th Anniversary of the bombardment of Fort McHenry in Baltimore harbor, the Coast Guard placed this buoy on the spot where Francis Scott Key was inspired to write the *Star Spangled Banner*.

Guard is generally associated with the automation of lights—because it presided over the final automation of aids to navigation—it is, in fact, quite possible that automation was, initially, slowed by the Coast Guard's 1939 takeover of the lighthouse establishment, especially on the Bay.

Though Putnam negotiated aggressively and successfully for improved employee benefits, in other ways his posture *vis à vis* his employees was bureaucratically detached. An interesting example is afforded in a brief comparison to the Lighthouse Board. When, in 1877, for example, the first portable libraries were distributed to lighthouse keepers, the Board waxed pious: "The moral effect of these libraries on the character of the keepers and their families can scarcely be too highly estimated."[10] In a curious way they also presaged the problem, if not the actual process, which shortly would begin to deprive keepers of their very occupation: "The books they contain," the report continued, "serve to keep their mental activity in operation and to prevent them from dwindling into mere machines, who finally come to perform their routine duties, as it were, by the system of automatic arrangement."[11]

113

Waterfront at Curtis Bay Yard, c. 1920

The CURTIS BAY Connection. The U.S. Coast Guard facility at Curtis Bay, near Baltimore, played an important part in the history of aids to navigation not only on the Chesapeake Bay but also on the nation's waterways. Originally a repair facility founded in 1899 by the Revenue Marine Service, it continues as the Coast Guard's only shipbuilding and repair facility. Today's Coast Guard was formed in1915 when the new department took over the functions of the Revenue Marine Service and the Lifesaving Service. Later, in 1939, the Lighthouse Service was merged with the Coast Guard and buoy construction began at the "depot," which it was called at the time.

When it was operated by the Revenue Marine Service, the depot at Arundel Cove (off Curtis Creek) was primarily a repair facility and home port for the fast cutters of its fleet. In 1906 sailors from the barque, *Chase* and the sidewheeler, *Colfax* built a small building on the shore to be used as a classroom to train Revenue Marine sailors. Previously instructions to Revenue Marine cadets was given on board the training ships, which had been sailing in New England. The 2-story shingle-framed school building built at Curtis Bay is considered the first home of the Coast Guard Academy. The main floor of the school building was used as a drill hall. Three classrooms were on the second floor and the loft was used for sail storage. The photo below shows the school building to the right with an officer's residence attached in later years. Other buildings at the time consisted of only a boat shed, a small carpentry shop and storage shed. The cadets lived onboard the *Chase* and the donated *Oriole*, a Maryland militia castoff. Later, the Naval Academy at Annapolis donated the training ship *Bancroft* for further cadet accommmodations. The first class of 5 cadets (shown below) graduated in 1906. In 1910 the "Academy" was moved to New London, Connecticut.

By then, the depot's building and repair facility had proven its worth to the newly formed Coast Guard. In 1940 at the onset of WWII, the depot was extensively expanded and the official designation was changed to a "Coast Guard Yard." Among Coast Guardsmen now it is simply refered to as "the Yard." Today, the Yard employs almost 800 civilian and military personel on 113 acres of land which include the shipyard, logistical support of the Coast Guard Fleet, homeport for activities such as navigational aids service, search and rescue, commercial licensing and ice-breaking for the Northern sector of the Bay, including management of the six small boat stations at Stillpond, Annapolis, Taylors Island, St.Inigoes and Crisfield, Maryland. The Yard is the homeport of the tender, *Red Birch* and the construction tender, *Sledge*.

Thirty one of Curtis Bay's early 20th century industrial buildings are listed in the National Register of Historic Places.

114

The Curtis Bay Yard built Lightship No. 612, the *Nantucket I*, the last U.S. lightship in service, and Lightship No. 613, her sistership the *Ambrose/Nantucket II* and the last lightship built in the U.S.

Every type of vessel from fiberglass 10' dinghys to oceangoing 255' cutters have been built at the Yard, including the following types and classes:

  2 - 255' cutters of the "Indian Tribes" class

  3 - 210' *Reliance* class cutters

  4 - 160' Inland construction tender

  5 - 157' Tenders, e.g. *Red Birch* and *Red Cedar*

  1 - 180' Tender *Ironwood* built 1943

  2 - 110' General purpose tugs

  37 - 95' Patrol boats, many used in Korean War

  53 - 82' Patrol boats used in Vietnam

  4 - 52' Steel motor lifeboats, 1956-1963

  3 - 52' Buoy boats,. built 1944

  15 - 46' Buoy boats with stern loading cranes

  14 - 45' Buoy boats built 1950s'

  110 - 44' Motor lifeboats built 1963-1972

  148 - 41' Utility boats

  300 - 40' Utility boats

  3 - 40' Buoy boats built 1940

  4 - 38' Duck amphibious boats built late 1940

  100 - T' type, 36' self righting motor life boats

  14 - 31' Port security boats

   Over 200-30' Utility boats.

In 1957 the Coast Guard introduced a small specialized type of workboat known as "buoy boats." Designed as auxiliary boats to the larger tenders, buoy boats were equipped with a lifting boom to handle small can and nun buoys. These tenders were able to work in tight quarters and shallow waters and generally assisted the larger tenders.

In 1944' the Yard constructed the 52' buoy boats shown above following the plans of a previous Lighthouse Service design. After WWII this type of small buoy tender was seen frequently on the Bay.

Among the many ships of the Coast Guard Fleet regularly maintain at the Yard today is the 295' cadet training barque, the *Eagle*.

All photos courtesy of Coast Guard Headquarters, Washington, D.C., the Curtis Bay Yard, Baltimore, Maryland, and the Coast Guard Academy, New London, Connecticut

Subchasers docked at the Yard after WWI, c.1920

Lighthouse Tender, LAUREL 1916-1930 The *Laurel* was a single-screw, steam-powered tender built in 1915 to Lighthouse Service plans at a cost of $55,502. At 105' overall, she was one of the smaller tenders designed for bay and sound work. Even so, her small crew of 4 officers and 12 men steamed 9,698 miles of the Chesapeake Bay and the Carolina coast in 1930 — 400 miles more than the larger *Holly*. She was apparently used so hard and sustained so much damage that she had to be retired in only 15 years.

The lighthouse establishment that Putnam inherited on the Chesapeake Bay was, in some respects, the largest and most complex lighthouse district in the country. The superintendent's office was in the Baltimore customs house, an arrangement that was becoming less and less satisfactory, for the Baltimore Harbor was ever more industrial and crowded with warehouses, a convoluted and competitive array of railroad spurs leading into the harbor (Baltimore never managed to create a union station), breweries, refineries and factories, including major steel mills. There was simply no land that could be purchased for consolidation or expansion of the administrative offices at the Lazaretto depot— nor was there sufficient space for docking, repair and receiving facilities. In fact, lighthouse tenders and vessels were usually berthed at nearby Curtis Bay. Added to this was the obvious logistical difficulty of having Fifth District headquarters in the upper Bay, a problem that had been addressed by the location of minor depots at intermediate points—Point Lookout, Alexandria, Annapolis, and Washington, as well as by the establishment of a major depot at Portsmouth. In many ways, it made more sense to administer the large Fifth District from the Virginia Capes (the district included, in addition to the Chesapeake Bay, Virginia's and North Carolina's seacoast lights and off-shore lightships, and extensive strings of North Carolina river lights). Putnam—described by one lighthouse historian as a "hard-driving, hard-working, two-fisted he-man"[12] — pushed Congress to appropriate land and money for the expansion of the Portsmouth depot facilities. In June of 1918, $275,000 had been authorized, but four years later an appropriation had yet to be made, and, in the end, the enlargement of this depot took more than a decade of effort.

The first delay was occasioned by the War Department's 1924 transfer of a site and buildings in Norfolk, Virginia, for purposes of building a new depot. Evidently the plans were scrapped, for the following year Putnam reported that "additional space adjoining the important depot at Portsmouth, Va., was purchased in order to permit extension of the wharves and buildings, and it is proposed to proceed with the work of construction as soon as the necessary approval of deed, etc., has been obtained."[13] In 1926, the much-needed remodeling was finally underway.[14] "The work consists in widening and dredging the slips, the reconstruction of the wharves, repairs and improvements to the old warehouse, and the construction of concrete roadways over the reservation."[15] It was estimated that the work would be completed in 1926—an estimate that was moved forward in each annual report. In fact, improvements were still being made in 1932, when the move of Fifth District head-quarters to this station was finally accomplished.[16] By this time, too, Harold D. King, who was to succeed Putnam as Commissioner of Lighthouses in 1937, had been promoted from his position as Superintendent of Lights in the Fifth District (a position he had held since 1915) to the Washington Bureau as Deputy Commissioner of Lights. The line of succession had been drawn.

Looking back over his career, Putnam felt that technical improvements were the hallmark of his administration at the Bureau of Lighthouses: "making use of radio, electricity, new illuminants, and improved fog signals."[17] Indeed, improvements followed improvements as, once again, the Lighthouse Service kept a squadron of personnel busily tinkering at the General Depot, trying to design the best apparatus for all navigational needs.

In 1922, Putnam was excited by the development of incandescent oil-vapor lamps, noting that they offered "a great increase of efficiency in the use of kerosene oil as an illuminant."[18] Not only did the incandescent oil vapor lamp provide an eight to ten-fold increase in illuminating power, but the savings in oil that obtained for lights of the first and second order was conspicuous, cutting kerosene consumption in half. But such savings were hardly measurable in the Bay's smaller fourth-order lights, and the change to incandescent oil-vapor was slow. Realistically, too, the increased brilliance of the light was not always needed at Bay lighthouses, and, thus, over the next decade, wick lamps

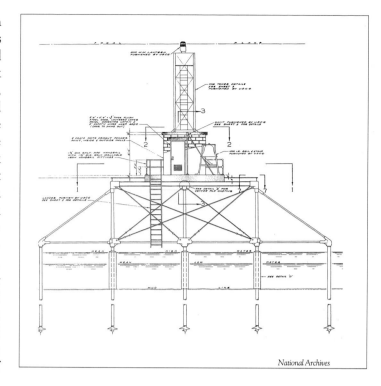

continued to be used in many attended light-houses. Ten years later, there were still twenty-one oil wick lamps in use—though by that time the use of electricity had greatly increased and dry-cell batteries were coming into use (as were "astronomical time clocks for turning on and off unwatched electric lights" and light sensitive photo-electric cells).[19] In 1932, $114,000 was spent on electrification in the Fifth District.[20]

Radio telephones were installed at various light stations, greatly lessening the isolation of keepers at remote locations. The installation of radio distance-finding stations also greatly improved safety, as did the possibilities of both ship-to-ship and ship-to-shore communication. Radio communication was undergoing constant improvement, for example, the synchronization of radio beacons by groups which eliminated interference between stations and improved the effectiveness of radio signals.

Like the oil-wick lamps, many of the Bay's 19th century, weight-driven bell machines and heavy cast-bronze fog bells were slow to be superseded. As late as 1932, there were still 41 clockwork fog signals in operation in the Fifth District. In these and other ways, inno-

The automatic light and fog bell at Tue Marshes, Virginia, is typical of the structures that replaced many screwpile lighthouses on the Bay

continued on page 121

117

Lighthouse Tenders MISLETOE & VIOLET were active tender on the Bay for almost 40 years. The *Mistletoe* was commissioned in1939 by the Pusey & Jones Shipyard, utilizing the same lines as the proven 1920 Lighthouse Service design of buoy tender so sucessful in bay and sound work. The 173' tender had an all steel hull with a steel and wood superstructure, and was powered by twin steam engines. The *Mistletoe* had two sisterships, the *Lilac* and the *Violet*. The *Violet* worked in the north Bay and was stationed at the Curtis Bay Yard in Baltimore, 1941-1962, while the *Mistletoe* worked primarily in southern Bay waters out of Portsmouth.

Lighthouse tenders such as the *Mistletoe* and the *Violet* performed a variety of tasks around the Bay besides tending buoys. The log of the *Mistletoe* showed the following activities for 1950-1963: September 1950, patrolled the President's Cup Regatta at Washington,D.C.; May 1951, assisted in dragging for downed plane near Langley Field; February 1953, refloated and towed the tug, Fortuna; July 1953, towed disabled CG patrol boat from Windmill Point Lighthouse to Portsmouth; January 1957, broke ice in the upper Potomac; January 1959, assisted the cutter *Madrona* aground at Point Lookout; August 1959, assisted in search for survivors following mid-air collision off Old Plantation Flats; September 1961, assisted two skin divers off Stingray Point; in March 1963, dragged for a downed Piper Cherokee airplane near Cape Henry.

The above photo of the *Mistletoe* shows her shortly after launching with the Lighthouse Service insignia on the bow. The color scheme of black hull, white superstructure, and buff mast and boom was retained by the Coast Guard. The dark hull color led Coast Guardsmen to refer to the tenders and work boats as the "black boats" of the service's fleet (versus the "white boats" for the cutters). Crews of the black boats are called "dungaree" sailors. The *Mistletoe* was decommissioned in 1968.

The photo opposite shows the crew of the *Violet* attempting to remove ice from a Bay buoy, a constant challenge for the tenders during the winter months on the Chesapeake Bay.

Lighthouse Tender NARCISSUS was launched with her sistership, the *Zinnia*, by the John H. Mathis Company, shipbuilders, Camden, New Jersey in 1939. She was 122' overall with a 27' beam and a 7' draft with twin 430 HP diesel engines. The *Narcissus* and her sistership were the first tenders to be built of extensive welded steel. The two ships' keels were laid before the Coast Guard takeover, using a Lighthouse Service design.

The *Narcissus* was originally assigned to Delaware and later stationed at Portsmouth to serve the lower Bay and the Carolina coast through WWII. She is shown below under construction at the Mathis Company shipyard with the *Zinnia* in the background. (The John Mathis Company was better known for its wooden pleasure yachts, including the presidential yacht *Sequoia*. The company was later renamed the John Trumpy & Sons Co. and moved to Annapolis, Maryland in 1947.)

119

LIGHTSHIP No. 101 served at Cape Charles, 1916-1924. She was built in 1916 by the Pusey & Jones shipyard of Wilmington, Delaware for $108,507. At 101' overall, with a 25' beam and a 11'4" draft, the ship was originally powered by a single 200 HP diesel engine capable of a speed of 8 knots. After leaving Cape Charles, No.101 went on to serve as a relief ship in the 5th District and, in 1926, was assigned to the Overfalls, Delaware station where she served until 1951. From 1951-1963 she was assigned to the Stonehorse Shoal, Massachusetts station. In 1964, No.101 was donated to the Portsmouth Lightship Museum in Portsmouth, Virgina, where she can still be seen in dry dock. Although no lightship station carried the name *Portsmouth*, No.101 was given the pseudo-name and the name was painted on her hull by the museum to impart a sense of place. Besides the *Chesapeake* (in Baltimore) and the *Portsmouth*, there are some 14 or 15 American lightships surviving in public displays. Many are open to the public.

*When a sailor gets to thinking
he is one the best.
Let him ship out on a lightship
and take the acid test.*

C. Tucker - lightship seaman, 1898

*All photos of lightship No.101 and her
crew courtesy of the Portsmouth
Museums, Lightship 101
Museum, Portsmouth, Virginia*

vation, except in the rapid acquisition of lighted buoys and river lights, was not a notable feature of the care given to aids to navigation—especially attended lights—on the Chesapeake Bay by the Bureau of Lighthouses.

There were, however, exceptions to the rule of an aging and shrinking lighthouse establishment on the Bay. In 1929, the "first synchronized radio beacon and air fog signal" was commissioned at Cape Henry, permitting navigators to estimate the station's distance without any special receiving equipment.[21] And the buoy depot at Lazaretto housed an important facility for the study of experimental fog signals and other devices, one of which, on the occasion of a speech given by President Harding near Fort McHenry, astonished all present by resounding impressively on a cloudless summer day. After a few moments of stunned bewilderment, it was determined that the automatic device had been triggered by the streams of water shooting across the harbor in honor of the president's visit.[22]

Of greatest importance, however, was the introduction of radio—making the maritime safety record of the U.S. lighthouse establishment one of the best in the world. Surprisingly, there was considerable resistance among mariners to its introduction, but Putnam, as always, responded with candor and aggressive measures to promote its use. "Only the radio signal," Putnam observed, "penetrates the fog and rain which may blot out a light, however brilliant; it alone is unaffected by the roar of the storm which drowns the sound of the most powerful signal."[23] By 1937, there were radio beacon installations—all of them distance-finding stations—on the following Chesapeake Bay light stations: Sandy Point, Cove Point, Smith Point, Cape Henry, Chesapeake Lightship, and Wolf Trap.

Another area of significant technological change during Putnam's long tenure at the Bureau of Lighthouses involved the realization of many improvements in the design of lightships. From the beginning, Putnam pushed hard for the enormous appropriations

Coast Guard

Workers at the Curtis Bay Yard maintained the lantern of the *Ambrose*, the last lightship built in the U.S.

necessary for construction of these new ships. By 1930, six state-of-the-art, diesel-powered ships had been built—ships that truly transformed lightship duty for the crews on stations lucky enough to receive one. "A single screw was driven by an electric motor; the current was generated by four Diesel sets which could be coupled together electrically for propulsion purposes or used separately to operate the auxiliary machinery."[24] Though very similar in outward appearance to the older ships, the pioneer ships could be underway in only a few minutes time, a definite plus in any emergency situation where propulsion was needed—for example, when a ship broke its moorings or needed engine power to stay on station during heavy seas. The lighter diesel equipment also meant a one-hundred-ton reduction in displacement, and the lessened resistance to the sea, in turn, meant much greater comfort for the ten-man crews that these ships originally held. Other comfort features included electric lights, air conditioning, and electrically operated pumps for running fresh and salt-water systems. The galleys were even "fitted with oil-burning

The concept of Experimental Lightship No. 99 came in the waning years of lightships, too late to ever be employed as an unmanned navigational aid.

ranges supplied with special coils for...hot water...and [had] provision for catching and filtering rain water."[25]

One of these ships, Lightship No. 116, was destined to be the last lightship to serve on the Chesapeake Bay.

The presidential order (part of Roosevelt's Reorganization Plan II), which in July of 1939 abolished the Bureau of Lighthouses and placed aids to navigation under the Coast Guard's jurisdiction, was, as one historian wryly noted, "a bolt out of the blue to all hands, but especially to the Bureau of Lighthouses in the Department of Commerce."[26] For one thing, the Bureau was immersed in preparations to celebrate one hundred fifty years of lighthouse service—and the big celebration, was only a month away. The testimonials were on everyone's lips, and there were even two books—Putnam's memoirs, published in 1937, and, fresh off the press, Irving Conklin's history of the Lighthouse Service. With congressional resolutions in place, commemorating the week of August 7 in honor of George Washington's signing of the first federal law relative to lighthouses in 1789, it hardly seemed possible that the Lighthouse Service—the oldest agency in the U.S.

government—could be eradicated with the stroke of a presidential pen. Disappointment is too mild a word to express the letdown, astonishment, alarm and confusion felt by the members of the Lighthouse Service—and, most assuredly, by the Navy (whose long association with the lighthouse establishment had been formalized before the Civil War, enshrined by the Lighthouse Board, and consolidated in times of war). There was no time for adjustment either; in Washington, the move to Coast Guard headquarters was accomplished in less than a week.

It has been suggested that the very decentralization of Putnam's organization—of which he was proud (though aware that it bucked the tide of official practice in Washington)—was the root cause of the transfer. It is true that in his 1937 memoirs, Putnam laments that "ever more centralization in Washington is the tendency."[27] Likewise, his successor as commissioner, Harold D. King, also made much of the Bureau's decentralized operations. Though surely he also meant to imply the bureaucratic efficiency of his organization, it has been suggested that his management style may have been perceived as too loose—especially since he was not yet afforded the same respect that Putnam's years in Washington had bestowed upon his office. With less than one percent of its personnel stationed in Washington, the Bureau's strategy may have backfired, implying instead that the district superintendents enjoyed too much autonomy, "with resultant lack of uniformity and economy."[28]

Whatever the reasons, the transfer placed an apprehensive—even hostile—group of civilian employees into a military service that at that time confronted many organizational challenges of its own. "In effect, a military service numbering 10,164 officers and men was to incorporate an organization comprising 4,119 full-time and 1,156 part-time employees, all of whom were civilians. Most of these were occupied in manning or maintaining some 30,000 aids to navigation, ranging from the more than 400 lighthouses and 30 lightships to the myriad unlighted buoys and shore marks, some of which were to be found in almost every harbor and navigable waterway in the United States and its possessions. ... The process of incorporating these civilians into the Coast Guard would not be the easier because few of them seem to have had any desire to accept military discipline and custom . . . ."[29]

Rules to govern the transfer of employees were set up, and these, to the great relief of many lighthouse keepers, offered important choices rather than summary dismissal. With some exceptions, the Lighthouse Service personnel were given the option of volunteering for induction into the Coast Guard or retention as civilian personnel. In the end, the split was about fifty-fifty. Though all ambivalence could not be smoothed over, the Coast Guard generally received high marks for its effort. In turn, they were pleasantly surprised by the discipline and competence of Lighthouse Bureau personnel. Lightship and tender duties, for example, proved to be far more rigorous and involved much greater skill than the Coast Guard had suspected.

On the Chesapeake Bay, many civilian keepers remained at their posts—some for over 20 years—and in these instances the vestiges of lighthouse families were sometimes preserved. But, formally at least, the lighthouse

The advanced technology that provided better, self-sustaining aids to navigation did not eliminate the need for constant maintainance of the buoys.

family had now ceased to exist. At first the lightship and tender crews tended to be unmixed, for the old seafarers of the Lighthouse Service were least appreciative of military bearing and most critical of the inexperience of many young Coast Guardsmen. But by the 1950s, both lighthouses and lightships often had mixed crews—each group adhering to the prescribed uniform, the civilian keeper sometimes cutting a rather somber figure in his gendarme-like dress suit. Though lighthouse duty, as it was now called, was dreaded by some young Coast Guardsmen, the stations were immaculately maintained—hence, many observers noted a marked improvement in the care of the Bay's light stations. Leave was generous—and so were food rations. Finally, the availability of telephones, radio and television all lessened the sense of isolation.

In the mid-1950s, the move to automation inevitably began to accelerate. Changes in regional ship-borne commerce and passenger traffic also had their effect. For most of the population, travel by automobile had supplanted travel by boat, and fewer and fewer residents were attuned to the Chesapeake's

123

The *White Pine* and her crew installed the atomic powered generator at Baltimore lighthouse in 1964.

Lighthouse Tender, WHITE PINE Although built in 1943, the *White Pine* is an efficient type of buoy tender still being used today. The all-steel construction of the tender is132' overall, with a 30' beam and 8'6" draft, powered by twin 600 HP diesel engines capable of a top speed of10.5 knots. Originally assigned to work on the Mississippi River, the tender spent 15 years on the Chesapeake Bay stationed at the Curtis Bay Yard. (She was later moved to the Gulf area and is still working buoys out of Mobile, Alabama.)

   Ironically, while many lighthouses and all lightships have become obsolete, the rarely celebrated tenders are still an important part of the aids-to-navigation system. Although helicopters are sometime used for the movement of small markers and rescue missions, nothing replaces the versatile buoy tender for overall maintainance and protection of the waterways. Their intrinsic value, now and in the past, has not escaped Coast Guard notice. In recognition of the unique vessel's contribution to the history of American lightkeeping, a new class of Coast Guard tenders known as the "Keeper Class" was recently introduced. Fourteen modern 175' coastal tenders will be built and named after lighthouse keepers, with the first of the new class, the *Ida Lewis*, launched in late1996.

shoreline and rivers. Additionally, as U.S. military presence continued to expand in and around the capital and in Hampton Roads, and as the Cold War occasioned fearful preoccupations with the strengthening of military defenses, the automation and demolition of old lighthouses did not always capture a great deal of attention. Apparently, at least two Chesapeake lighthouses were accidentally destroyed in Navy target practice. Sharp-shooters and vandals on the Bay also began to contribute their share of damage to the unattended light stations while tended light stations continued to dwindle in number.

Over the years, the accumulation of lightship disasters (especially the loss of life in the 1934 sinking of Lightship No. 117 on Nantucket sound) was deeply disturbing to lighthouse administrators and convinced many that an automated lightship was the best and final solution in lightship design. In 1949, the U.S. Coast Guard began research on Lightship No. 99, an experimental, unmanned vessel that was modified at the Coast Guard's Curtis Bay boat yards. At this time, it was considered "a unique and daring departure," bringing the inevitable automation of all navigational aids within reach. "Not a soul," one observer noted, "will be aboard it; all orders will be executed by electronic henchmen controlled from a switchboard. ... From a radar set at its masthead the operator ashore can watch nearby ship traffic and can also tell if the ship has been pulled off station."[30]

Ninety-one feet in length, with a displacement of 215 tons, the ship contained no propulsion machinery. Instead, the four diesel generators were meant to rotate operation on a three-month schedule, each one providing sufficient power to operate the ship's up-to-date equipment, including a fog signal composed of one hundred eighty individual loudspeakers—though, from an earlier era, a 1,000-pound bronze bell with an automatic striker was placed on the foredeck, poised to sound in case of loudspeaker failure. The savings in construction and maintenance costs was thought to be more than half the cost of a manned lightship—and that before the crew salaries were figured in.[31]

Thus, on the Chesapeake Bay, the lighthouse establishment had curiously come full circle. At the same time, however, other design engineers looked to the Mexican Gulf, "where oil drillers [had] performed miracles in building apparently wave and wind-proof derrick structures over off-shore wells...." These "permanent islands," it was correctly observed, might render all lightships obsolete.[32]

Today, the Coast Guard's *Light List* defines a lighthouse as an "historic structure"—omitting mention of any navigational importance, past or present. Thus, in a real sense, it may be said that the lighthouse has disappeared, following the keepers into oblivion. In fact, however, since the late 1960s, a widespread nostalgia for the days of lightkeepers and for the old lighthouses themselves has awakened historical sensibilities that have found voice in the efforts of local groups and the energy of regional museums. Though it has not been too long ago that one Coast Guard commander could smartly proclaim that, "We are not in the business of maintaining historic structures," in point of fact, today's Coast Guard, for reasons of its own,

Coast Guard

has become an enthusiastic member of the lighthouse preservation movement. "The Coast Guard," a Fifth-District lieutenant recently explained to the members of the Chesapeake Chapter of the U.S. Lighthouse Society, "manages lighthouses under the blanket of two mandates. The first is our fundamental requirement to provide Aids to Navigation to the mariner. The other mandate is the National Historic Preservation Act."[33] Though noting that the Act "does not specifically prohibit adverse actions against historic structures, it does lay out clear guidance for Coast Guard consultation with state historic preservation officers before taking any action."[34] Today's Coast Guard is quick to note the affection and symbolic importance that reside with the Bay's remaining lighthouses. In fact, it may now be—just possibly —a safe bet that no other Chesapeake Bay lighthouse will be lost.

In 1965, the last active lightship on the Bay, No. 116, the *Chesapeake* leaves her station for the last time. She was replaced by a "Texas tower" lighthouse — the last lighthouse built on the Bay.

125

Designed by
EASTWIND PUBLISHING
Annapolis, Maryland

Collection, P. Hornberger

END NOTES

INTRODUCTION
1 Alice Jane Lippson, editor, *The Chesapeake Bay in Maryland* (Baltimore, Maryland: The Johns Hopkins University Press, 1973), p. 2.
2 Arthur Pierce Middleton, *Tobacco Coast: A Maritime History of the Chesapeake Bay in the Colonial Era* (Baltimore: Johns Hopkiins University Press, 1984, @ The Mariner's Museum, 1953), p. 43.
3 Alice Jane Lippson, op. cit.
4 Ibid, p. 10; Arthur Pierce Middleton, op. cit., p. 63.

CHAPTER ONE
1 Frederick Gutheim, *The Potomac* (Baltimore and London: The Johns Hopkins University Press, 1986, @ 1949).
2 Frederick Tilp, *This Was Potomac River* (@ by Frederick Tilp, 1978) p. 90. This unhappy, but not unusual, circumstance led to the placement of the Potomac's first river buoy, carried to its position by the Norfolk buoy tender *Polly & Sally* in June of 1793, one year after the commissioning of the Cape Henry light.
3 Ibid.
4 Arnold B. Johnson, *The Modern Lighthouse Service* (Washington, D.C.: Government Printing Office, 1889), p. 14.
5 Tilp, op. cit., p. 94. See, also, Carl Bode, *Maryland: A History* (New York: W.W. Norton & Company, 1978), pp. 53-54. *Rear Admiral George Cockburn entered the Chesapeake in February of 1813 and set up a blockade. In April, when all danger of ice had passed, he sailed up the Bay to Havre de Grace ("menacing Baltimore and Annapolis" along the way) where his troops wreaked havoc on the town, plundering and burning two-thirds of the homes. When the British began firing newly designed rockets on the town, most of the militia fled to the hinterland in terror, leaving the town to be defended by John O'Neill (whose heroism later won for him the position as first lightkeeper at Concord Point). Looting was rampant. "The officers picked out tables and bureaus that they liked, wrote their names on them, and had them put aboard the British barges. Admiral Cockburn himself coveted an elegant coach he saw and ordered it hauled aboard his vessel." Soon joined on the Chesapeake by another British fleet, "the combined forces scattered over both the Eastern and Western shores, marauding at will." Washington, however, was thought to be inaccessible to the British warships, as Captain Charles Napier; speaking of the British effort to reach Washington in 1813 observed. "Nature has done much for the protection of this country's capital city, by placing, one-third of the way up, very extensive and intricate shoals, called Kettle Bottoms. They are composed of oyster banks of various dimension, some no larger than a boat, with passages between them." That spring, two British frigates bombarded Fort Washington (then Fort Warburton), dangerously close to the capital, and much to the surprise and later disgrace of the fort's commander, Captain Samuel T. Dyson, who was court-martialed and discharged for hastily detonating the fort's ammunition stores and calling his men to abandon the fort.*
6 The spelling of Pleasonton's name varies from book to book—and sometimes within the same document—appearing as well as *Pleasanton*.
7 Francis Ross Holland, Jr. *America's Lighthouses* (New York: Dover Publications, Inc., 1988, @ 1972), pp. 30-31.
8 Clio Group, Inc. and John M. Adams, *Historic Structures Report for the Keeper's House, Concord Point Lighthouse, Havre de Grace, Maryland* (prepared for The Friends of Concord Point Lighthouse and The Maryland Historical Trust, October, 1990), p. 20.
9 We have taken the spelling of Donahoo's name from family tombstones that appear in the Havre de Grace cemetery, though other spellings (for example, Donohoo and Donohue) may be found in archival materials and appear to have been used by him as well.
10 From the original minutes of the Town of Havre de Grace, referenced in correspondence between an officer of the Friends of Concord Point Lighthouse, to L. Donahoo-Hatchell, June 6, 1991.
11 Clio Group, Inc. and John M. Adams, op. cit., p. 7.
12-18 Richard W. Updike, "Winslow Lewis and the Lighthouses," *The American Neptune*, 28, 1968: 31-48. Updike writes (p.31) that Lewis "was canny and he was crafty; moreover, there is evidence to suggest that when circumstances were propitious,, he could even indulge in a little sharp practice...but he was not without merit also. He was inventive and resourceful, and...he was able, by observation and practical experience, to patent a superior method of lighthouse illumination, as well as to become the nation's foremost lighthouse designer and builder. His contribution to the safety of navigation in North America is a debt which an ungrateful government has never properly acknowledged."
19 Clio Group, Inc. and John M. Adams, op. cit. pp. 7-8.
20 Ibid; also, Richard W. Updike, op. cit., pp. 43-44.
21 Stephen Pleasonton, May 24, 1851 to William L. Hodge, Acting Secretary of the Treasury, in *Report of the Officers Constituting the Light-House Board, Convened Under Instructions from the Secretary of the Treasury to Inquire into the Condition of the Light-House Establishment of the United States, Under the Act of March 3, 1851* (Washington: A. Boyd Hamilton, 1852).
22-23 *Report of the Officers Constituting the Light-House Board*, op. cit.
24 The Clio Group and John M. Adams, op. cit.
25 *Annual Report of the Light-House Board*, op.cit., 1894, p. 232; also, Arnold B. Johnson, op.cit.
26 *Annual Report of the Light-House Board*, op.cit. 1894.
27 Frederick Tilp, op. cit., p. 92.
28 Stephen Pleasonton, quoted in *Report of the Officers Constituting the Light-House Board*, op. cit.
29 Frederick Tilp, op. cit., pp. 99-109.
30 Hans Christian Adamson, *Keepers of the Lights* (New York: Greenberg Publisher, 1955), p. 40.
31 Willard Flint, *Lightships of the United States Government: Reference Notes* (Washington, D.C.: The Coast Guard Historian's Office, 1989), no page numbers.
32 Frederick Tilp, op. cit. pp. 110-121.
33 Willard Flint, op. cit.
34 W.J. Hardy, *Lighthouses: Their History and Romance* (New York: Fleming H. Revell Company, 1896) p. 72. Hardy tells an interesting story about the business deals that surrounded placement of these first lightships. *"We do not hear of another proposal for floating lights at the Nore till 1730. Robert Hamblin had then devised a scheme for getting the whole of the lighting of the English coast into his own hands. ... His plan was to fix floating lights at short distances from the shore, in such positions as would render the existing lighthouses absolutely useless. It was a bold stroke, and so far successful that he actually got his patent from the crown and established some of his lights, amongst them that at the Nore. But his reign was short; the Trinity House addressed a powerful remonstrance to the law officers of the crown, the owners of private lighthouses joined in the complaint, and Hamblin's patent was speedily cancelled. But before the cancelling he had parted with any rights he possessed under his general patent with regard to the lightships at the Nore and at one or two other points, and in 1732, the purchaser, David Avery, placed a lightship at the east end of the Nore Sands. After circulating in shipping circles very glowing accounts of the benefits which this light would yield to navigation, he began to ask for his tolls, and by a little judicious dealing with the Trinity House he managed to get that body on his side. ... He arranged that the Trinity House should itself apply for a new patent from the crown...and that he should take a lease of this patent, when granted for a term of sixty-one years at a yearly rent of 100 [pounds sterling]. ... Avery must have made a good profit."*
35 Willard Flint, op. cit.; Hans Christian Adamson, op. cit. p. 42.
36 W.J. Hardy, op. cit.
37 On September 2, 1819, a contract was awarded to James Poole of Hampton, Virginia with specifications that the vessel be *"70 tons burthen, copper fastened and coppered...a cabin with at least four berths...apartment for cooking, spars, a capstan belfry, yawl and davids [sic]."* Quoted in Flint, op. cit.
38 Ibid. "Early light vessels," Flint writes, "were largely a product of opin-ion and arbitrary judgment on the part of builders who were often ignorant of

the true purpose of the vessel or its harsh operating environment."

39 George R. Putnam, Sentinel of the Coasts: The Log of a Lighthouse Engineer (New York: W.W. Norton & Company, 1937), pp. 195-196.

40-41 Willard Flint, op. cit.

42 Gustav Kobbe, "Life on the South Shoal Lightship," in Charles Nordhoff, The Light-Houses of the United States in 1874 (Silverhome, CO: Vista Books, 1993), pp. 35-47.

43 George R. Putnam, *Lighthouses and Lightships of the United States* (Boston and New York: Houghton Mifflin Company, 1917) pp. 204.

44-48 See, Willard Flint, op. cit. See, also, *Report of the Officers Constituting the Light-House Board*, op. cit.

49 Frederick Tilp, op. cit., p. 99.

50 Ibid, p. 108.

51 Ibid, pp. 95-109.

52-60 *Report of the Officers Constituting the Light-House Board*, op. cit.

CHAPTER TWO

1 Francis Ross Holland, Jr., *America's Lighthouses* (New York: Dover Pblications, Inc., 1988, @ 1972), p. 34. "It is doubtful," Holland writes, "that any agency prior to that time, or, perhaps, subsequently, went through such a searching inspection."

2 Charles Nordhoff, "The Lighthouses of the United States" (Silverthorne, Colorado: Vistabooks Publishing, 1993,@ Harper's Magazine, 1872), p. 10.

3 Ibid, p. 17.

4 Francis Ross Holland, Jr., op. cit., p. 36.

5-6 Arnold B. Johnson, *The Modern Light-House Service* (Washington, D.C.: Government Printing Office, 1889) pp. 21-23.

7-8 Charles Nordhoff, op. cit., p. 16.

9-10 Edward P. Adams, "The Lighthouse System of the United States," transcript of a paper read January 25, 1893 at the Association of Engineering Societies.

11 Frederick Gutheim, *The Potomac* (Baltimore and London: The Johns Hopkins University Press, 1986, @ 1949), p. 295.

12 Philip Van Doren Stern, *The Confederate Navy: A Pictorial History* (New York: Da Capo Press, 1992, @ 1962), pp. 15-17.

13-14 Carl Bode, *Maryland: A History* (New York and London: W.W. Norton & Co., 1978) p. 123.

15 Daniel Carroll Toomey, *The Civil War in Maryland* (Baltimore, MD: Toomey Press, 1996, @ 1983), p. 12; Carl Bode, op. cit., pp. 121-126.

16 Daniel Carroll Toomey, op. cit.

17 Ibid, p. 21.

18-19 Philip Van Doren Stern, op. cit., pp. 7-8.

20 Daniel Carroll Toomey, op. cit., p. 34.

21 "Operations on the Potomac and Rappahannock Rivers," Dec. 7, 1861, to July 31, 1865, *Naval Official Records*.

22 Ibid.

23 Frederick Tilp, *This Was Potomac River* (@ by Frederick Tilp, 1978) p.95; also, Joseph Norris, "St. Clement's Island, Witness to American History," in publication for the 27th Historical Pageant and Blessing of the Fleet, October, 1994, pp. 31-43.

24 Frederick Gutheim, op. cit., pp. 295-97; 315-16.

CHAPTER THREE

1 Frederick Tilp, *This Was Potomac River* (@ by Frederick Tilp, 1978) p.188.

2 Charles Nordhoff, *The Lighthouses of the United States* (Silverthorne, Colorado: Vistabooks Publishing,1993, @ Harper's Magazine, 1872), p. 17.

3-5 Arnold B. Johnson, *The Modern Light-House Service* (Washington, D.C.: Government Printing Office, 1889), pp. 104-5.

6-10 The Light-House Board, *Instructions to Light-Keepers and Masters of Light-House Vessels* (Washington, D.C.: Government Printing Office, 1902, reproduced in facsimile by the Great Lakes Lighthouse Keepers Association, 1989), pp. 5-15.

11-13 *The Annual Report of the Light-House Board* (Washington, D.C.: Government Printing Office, 1877), pp. 4-5.

14 David Porter Heap, *Ancient and Modern Lighthouses* (Boston: Ticknor and Company, 1889), pp. 186-199.

15 *The Annual Report of the Light-House Board* (Washington, D.C.: Government Printing Office, 1895), pp. 99-100.

16 *The Annual Report of the Light-House Board*, op. cit., 1877, p.6.

17 *The Annual Report of the Light-House Board*, 1886, pp.133-138.

18-22 *The Annual Report of the Light-House Board*, 1894, pp. 229-230.

23 One Light-House Board member, who cheerfully undertook a straightforward description of the process from lighthouse proposal to Congressional appropriation, offers a fair understanding of why the Board's popularity in government circles was lagging. "*Each light-house is established by Congressional enactment. A petition from those interested, usually ship-owners and ship-masters, is presented by the Representative in Congress in whose Congressional district it is proposed that the light-house should be located. The House of Representatives or Senate refers the petition to its Committee on Commerce, which asks the opinion of the Secretary of the Treasury on the matter. He refers the question to the Light-House Board, which in turn calls on the inspector and engineer of the proper light-house district to examine and report on the necessity, practicability, and cost of the proposed structure. Their reports, with such other information on the subject as the Board may have at hand, is referred to its own committee on location, when a formal report and recommendation is made to the Board, which report is transmitted to the Secretary of the Treasury, who in turn sends both his own opinion and the Board's recommendation of the committee of the Senate or lower House, asking the information, and on the report of that committee, if it is favorable, is based the report of the Committee on Appropriations and the action of Congress. But frequently the reports are unfavorable, and it has happened that the Board has been interpolated on the same matter by several successive Congresses, and has been required to build the light-house it has reported was not needed.*" (Arnold B. Johnson, op. cit., pp. 109-110.)

24 George R. Putnam, *Sentinel of the Coasts: The Log of a Lighthouse Engineer* (New York: W.W. Norton & Company, 1937) p. 158.

CHAPTER FOUR

1-6 *Annual Report of the Commissioner of Lighthouses* (Washington: Government Printing Office, 1922), p. 3-5.

7-8 *Annual Report of the Commissioner of Lighthouses*, op. cit., 1925, pp. 1-2.

9 *Annual Report of the Commissioner of Lighthouses*, op. cit., 1932, p.16.

10-11 *Annual Report of the Light-House Board* (Washington, D.C.: Government Printing Office, 1877), p. 7.

12 Hans Christian Adamson, *Keepers of the Lights* (New York: Greenberg Publisher, 1955), p. 29.

13 *Annual Report of the Commissioner of Lighthouses*, op. cit., 1925, p.12

14 *Annual Report of the Commissioner of Lighthouses*, op. cit., 1926, p. 8. Putnam points out that the depot was home to no less than "twelve tenders and lightships."

15 Ibid, p. 6 (see, also, p. 25).

16 *Annual Report of the Commissioner of Lighthouses*, op.cit., 1928, p.28.

17 George R. Putnam, *Sentinel of the Coasts: The Log of a Lighthouse Engineer* (New York: W.W. Norton & Company, 1937) p. 164.

18 *Annual Report of the Commissioner of Lighthouses*, op. cit., 1922, p. 6.

19 *Annual Report of the Commissioner of Lighthouses*, op. cit., 1932, p. 2.

20 Ibid, p. 25.

21 Ibid, 1929, p. 5.

22 Hans Christian Adamson, op. cit., p. 367.

23 G.R. Putnam, op. cit.1937, p. 200.

24 Hans Christian Adamson, op. cit., pp. 46-47.

25 Ibid.

26 Ibid, p. 30.

27 George R. Putnam, 1937, pp. 155-156.

28 Robert Erwin Johnson, *Guardians of the Sea: A History of the United States Coast Guard, 1915 to the Present* (Annapolis, Maryland: Naval Institute Press, 1987), p. 161.

29 Ibid.

30-31 H.C. Adamson, op. cit., p. 51.

32 Ibid, pp. 51-52.

33 Lieutenant Edward A. Westfall, in a speech to the Chesapeake Chapter of the United States Lighthouse Society, December 7, 1996, Arlington, Virginia.

34 Ibid.

BIBLIOGRAPHY

Adamson, Hans Christian *Keepers of the Lights*. New York: Greenberg Publisher, 1955.

Angle, Paul M. *A Pictorial History of the Civil War Years*. New York: Main Street Books, Doubleday, 1980 (c. 1967).

Boatner, Mark M., III. *The Civil War Dictionary*. New York: David McKay Company, Inc., revised edition, 1987.

Bode, Carl. *Maryland: A History*. New York: W.W. Norton & Company, 1978.

Brouwer, Norman J. *International Register of Historic Ships*. Peekskill, New York: Sea History Press, National Maritime Historical Society, 1993.

Burgess, Robert H. *This Was Chesapeake Bay*. Cambridge, Maryland: Cornell Maritime Press, Inc. 1963.

Burgess, Robert H. *Chesapeake Circle*. Cambridge, Maryland: Cornell Maritime Press, Inc., 1965.

Canfield, Eugene B. *Notes on Naval Ordnance of the American Civil War, 1861-1865*. Washington, D.C.: The American Ordnance Association, 1960.

Cohen, Richard Bowman. "Once There Was Light," *Virginia Cavalcade*, Summer, 1977, pp. 5-19.
de Gast, Robert. *The Lighthouses of the Chesapeake*. Baltimore and London: The Johns Hopkins University Press, 1973.

Flint, Willard. *Lightships of the United States Government: Reference Notes*. Washington, D.C.: The Coast Guard Historian's Office, 1989.

Floherty, John J. *Men Without Fear*. New York: J.B. Lippincott Company, 1941.

Gutheim, Frederick *The Potomac*. Baltimore and London: The Johns Hopkins University Press, 1986, @ 1949.

Heap, David Porter. *Ancient and Modern Lighthouses*. Boston: Ticknor and Company, 1889 (c. 1886).
Hoffman, Frederick J. *The Twenties*. New York: The Free Press, 1962 (c. 1949).

Holland, Francis Ross, Jr. *America's Lighthouses*. New York: Dover Publications, Inc., 1988, @ 1972.

Holland, Francis Ross. *Maryland Lighthouses of the Chesapeake Bay*. Crownsville, Maryland: The Maryland Historical Trust Press and The Friends of St. Clement's Island Museum, Inc., Colton's Point Maryland, 1997.

Holly, David C. *Chesapeake Steamboats*. Centreville, Maryland: Tidewater Publishers, 1994.

Holly, David C. *Tidewater by Steamboat, A Saga of the Chesapeake*. Baltimore and London: The Johns Hopkins University Press, 1991 (published in association with The Calvert Marine Museum).

Johnson, Arnold B. *The Modern Light-House Service*. Washington: Government Printing Office, 1889.

Johnson, Robert Erwin. *Guardians of the Sea: A History of the United States Coast Guard, 1915 to the Present*. Annapolis, Maryland: Naval Institute Press, 1987.

Kobbe, Gustav. "Life on the South Shoal Lightship," *The Lighthouses of the United States*. Silverthorne, CO: Vistabooks Publishing, 1993 (reprinted from *Century Magazine*, 1894).

Lippson, Alice Jane. Editor. *The Chesapeake Bay in Maryland: An Atlas of Natural Resources*. Baltimore and London: The Johns Hopkins University Press, 1973.

Middleton, Arthur Pierce *Tobacco Coast*. Baltimore and London: The Johns Hopkins University Press and The Maryland Archives, 1984.

Nordhoff, Charles. *The Lighthouses of the United States*. Silverthorne, CO: Vistabooks Publishing, 1993 (reprinted from *Harpers*, Vol. 38, March, 1874).

Putnam, George R. *Lighthouses and Lightships of the United States*. Boston and New York: Houghton Mifflin Company, 1917.

Putnam, George R. *Sentinel of the Coasts*. New York: W.W. Norton & Company, 1937.

Roberts, Bruce, and Ray Jones. *Western Lighthouses*. Old Saybrook, Connecticut: The Globe Pequot Press, 1993.

BIBLIOGRAPHY

Scheina, Robert L. *U.S. Coast Guard Cutters & Craft, 1946-1990*. Annapolis, Maryland: Naval Institute Press, 1990.

Scheina, Robert L. *U.S. Coast Guard Cutters & Craft of World War II*. Annapolis, Maryland: Naval Institute Press, 1982.

Shagena, Jack L. *Brief History & Walking Tour of Historic Chesapeake City, Maryland*. Chesapeake City, Maryland: Jack L. Shagena, 1996.

Stern, Philip Van Doren *The Confederate Navy*. New York: DaCapo Press, 1992, @ 1962.

Talbot, Frederick A. *Lightships and Lighthouses*. Philadelphia: J.B. Lippincott Company, 1913.

Tilp, Frederick. *This Was Potomac River*. @ by Frederick Tilp, 1978.

Toomey, Daniel Carroll. *The Civil War in Maryland*. Baltimore, Maryland: Toomey Press, 1983.

Turbyville, Linda *Bay Beacons*. Annapolis, Maryland: Eastwind Publishing, 1995.

GOVERNMENT PUBLICATIONS & ARCHIVES

Record Group No. 26. Records of the U.S. Coast Guard and its predecessors, The Bureau of Lighthouses and the U.S. Light-House Board. The National Archives of the United States, Washington, D.C.

The Bureau of Lighthouses *Annual Report of the Commissioner of Lighthouses*. Washington: Government Printing Office, 1911-1932.

The Light-House Board *Annual Reports of the Light-House Board*. Washington: Government Printing Office, 1852-1910.

The Light-House Board. *List of Lights and Fog Signals*. Washington: Government Printing Office, 1896.

The Light-House Board. *Report of the Officers Constituting the Light-House Board, Convened Under Instructions from the Secretary of the Treasury to Inquire into the Condition of the Light-House Establishment of the United States, Under the Act of March 3, 1851*. Washington: A. Boyd Hamilton, 1852.

NOTE: In addition to works cited, the authors have relied on information provided by many individuals and archival materials available at The Archives of the United States, Washington, D.C. and Philadelphia, Pennsylvania; The U.S. Coast Guard Headquarters, Washington, D.C.; The U.S. Coast Guard, Fifth District Headquarters, Portsmouth, Virginia; The Library of Congress, Washington, D.C.; The Enoch Pratt Library, Baltimore, Maryland; Maryland Hall of Archives, Annapolis, Maryland; The Chesapeake Bay Maritime Museum, St. Michaels, Maryland; The Calvert Marine Museum, Solomons, Maryland; The Mariners' Museum, Newport News, Virginia; The Nimitz Library, U.S. Naval Academy, Annapolis, Maryland.

INDEX

INDEX

133

INDEX

~